Snapshots of Instructional Supervision

Reflections of Scholars in the Field

Helen M. Hazi
Maria Piantanida, Editors

Wisdom of Practice Series

Learning Moments Press
Oakmont, PA

Snapshots of Instructional Supervision:
Reflections of Scholars in the Field
Published by Learning Moments Press
Oakmont, PA 15139
Learningmomentspress.com

ISBN-13 979-8-9860800-5-5
BISAC Subject: Education/Administration/School
Superintendents & Principals (EDU001040)
Education/Collaborative & Team Teaching (EDU050000)
Education/Computers & Technology (EDU039000)
Education/Cultural Pedagogies (EDU62000)
Education/Policy/Reform/General (EDU034000)
Education/Evaluation/Assessment (EDU011000)
Education/Leadership (EDU032000)
Education/Professional Development (EDU046000)
Education/Rural (EDU052000)
Education/Teacher Training & Certification (EDU053000)

Onix audience Code: 06 Professional & Scholarly

Book Layout
Mike Murray, pearhouse.com

Through the years, the deliberations of COPIS members and the discourses of supervision have been enriched by the contributions of scholars who are no longer living. If it is true that what we are able to accomplish today is because we stand on the shoulder of giants, then we owe a debt of gratitude to the scholars who came before us. The work we continue to do today and into tomorrow honors their legacy.

Table of Contents

Foreword

John Smyth

John Smyth is Emeritus Research Professor, Federation University Australia. He is a Fellow of the Academy of the Social Sciences in Australia, a former Senior Fulbright Research Scholar, and the recipient of several awards from the American Educational Research Association for his critical ethnographic work. He has been a university academic for 51 years and is the author/editor of over 40 books and more than 300 scholarly papers. He is a sociologist who has worked on a variety of aspects of critical sociology and social justice. Among his most recent books is *The Toxic University: Zombie Leadership, Academic Rock Stars, and Neoliberal Ideology* (Palgrave Macmillan). John is also the founder and current series editor of the *Palgrave Critical University Studies* series. In retirement, when he is not travelling, John has turned to writing local social history of his home town, Ballarat, Australia, and has recently published a book entitled *Johnny Allloo of Ballarat Notoriety* (Published by the Xin Jin Shan Chinese Library, Ballarat) on one of the first Chinese immigrants to come to Australia in 1844, before the Australian gold rush. The book is important because it reveals the beginnings of the White Australia Policy, which was a discriminatory racist policy directed at immigrants that lasted in Australia up until 1973. The subject of the book was also a pioneering restaurateur with the advertising motif "soups always ready" in 1853, arguably making him the pioneer of takeaway food!

B efore I get started, I need to do a little bit of context setting, and as sociologists say (and I am one of them), context is everything!

Marx made a very prescient comment in 1852, when he said—and I am paraphrasing here—"we make our own history, but not the circumstances under which it is made." This idea, seems to apply well to the history of COPIS. While those of us who belong/have belonged to COPIS (and I joined in 1985, after being introduced to the group by Noreen Garman in 1983 in Houston via an invited lecture), have burrowed away at our scholarship, the conditions under which we did it were not always that helpful to the flourishing of COPIS or the field of supervision as a field of study. I will give an example of what I mean. The "enforced" marriage (or at least that is what it seemed like to me) between "supervision" and "curriculum" through the *Journal of Curriculum and Supervision* was not a particularly happy marriage for those of us who were looking for a publication outlet for our scholarship on supervision. This unhappy marriage ended rather disastrously in 2005 with the cessation of that publication.

From my vantage point of a 20,000-mile round trip from Australia to the US, this heralded the death knell to my 20 something year career in supervision, made even more terminal by the fact that no such field of scholarship exists in the Antipodes—the nearest we have to supervision is "inspection," which has all manner of negative connotations. I was already an enforced refugee from the inhospitable and moribund field of educational administration, and the only glimmer of hope I had looked to, was being extinguished. My last attendance at COPIS was in 2005 and that was because I held an endowed chair at Texas State University and travel was feasible.

But there was much more involved than just an appropriate publication outlet. Somewhat ironically, I addressed the underlying issue in a paper I wrote that was published in the *Teachers College Record* of Summer 1987 (a revision of a paper I had presented at San Francisco AERA in the previous year, 1986). In retrospect, I believe I accurately nailed the problem in the title of my paper—"The Cinderella Syndrome: A Philosophical View of Supervision as a Field of Study."

I strongly believed then, as I do now, that supervision is indeed a very legitimate field of study. In invoking the fairy tale motif of Cinderella, what I was alluding to was the second-class way in which the field of supervision was perceived more widely. Like in the fairytale, I believe that supervision has been malevolently treated by its "stepfather" [sic], the scientific field of educational administration, but through benevolent intent and the assiduous hard work of scholars in organizations like COPIS, it has re-invented itself in no small way by creating a dedicated outlet in the form of the *Journal of Educational Supervision* and monographs like this one.

While supervision may have been forced to, as Helen Hazi (2019) so eloquently put it, travel "incognito" through no fault of its own, in its struggle for visibility, that is now hopefully all in the past. The field is now poised to head in a much more vibrant and hopeful direction, and documents like this are testament to that trajectory. I can think of no other field of study in education that has been as thoughtful, introspective, and reflective than the field of supervision—and the "think pieces" contained herein are a tangible manifestation of that.

I regard it as a sign of intellectual health that a field of study is not settled or smugly self-satisfied, but rather is always restless and disruptive, sometimes even in turmoil, continually asking itself the question "what are we up to?" When things become settled and too comfortable intellectually, they atrophy and die—that is certainly not the case with educational supervision!

I thoroughly congratulate all of those involved in bringing this document into existence and highly recommend it to anyone interested in the field of supervision.

Preface

Helen M. Hazi & Maria Piantanida

Background

At the fall 2022 conference of COPIS, Ian Mette challenged members to consider making *critical* supervision central to the organization's purpose so that it might become more in tune with the current educational landscape. While some members shared this view, others questioned it. As the fall 2023 conference approached Helen Hazi and Ian Mette thought it would be useful to continue the conversation. Therefore, they invited COPIS members to share reflections on the evolution of the field of instructional supervision by considering the questions: Who is Instructional Supervision Intended to Serve? How does Instructional Supervision function?

Reflections might also address definition(s) of supervision, its purposes, challenges, boundaries, current issues, and its past and future as a field of study and practice. Submissions were in the form of think pieces that were circulated in advance of a conversational session held at the fall 2023 COPIS conference in Boise, Idaho.

Following the conference, the idea of collecting the think pieces into a monograph emerged. In addition to those who had submitted think pieces prior the conference, an invitation was again extended to all COPIS members to submit a think piece. The result is this collection, *Snapshots of Instructional Supervision: Reflections of Scholars in the Field*.

Rationale for the Monograph

As the title suggests, this monograph is not an exhaustive or systematic review of issues in the field of supervision. Rather, like snapshots in a family photo album, the think pieces offer glimpses into the authors' concerns about the field of supervision within this particular historical moment. Among the concerns are perennial issues of identity, stigma, terminology, and purpose of supervision. More current concerns focus on issues of cultural inclusiveness, social justice, and the impact of rapidly changing technology. As a whole, the monograph provides a composite (albeit momentary) memory of supervision as a field of study.

A *field of study*, as Pinar et al. (1995) remind us, is "a tradition of language or discourse" (p. 7) that develops over time. Supervision has been a field of study since the early 19th century, and COPIS members, as inhabitants of this field, have witnessed its evolution over nearly 50 years. The field has experienced its "golden age" in the 1980s (Garman, 2020), wrestled with school reform mandates in the 1990s (e.g., Sullivan, 2016), and had a tumultuous relationship with teacher evaluation in the 1990s and beyond (e.g., Gordon, 1992).

All fields of study "have histories, all evolve, all suffer 'paradigm' breaks, and all proceed in directions they might not have, had those who devoted their careers to these fields not existed" (Pinar et al.,1995, p. 849). Despite its peaks and valleys, supervision as a field of study lives on when scholars use its name and cite its many past and present scholars. A monograph such as this one serves as an historical artifact that records something of the discourses that continue to shape the field.[1]

Significance of COPIS

As Pinar et al. suggest, fields of study are shaped by scholars who care enough to engage in discourses about common concerns. COPIS, founded in 1975, represents such a discourse community and provides a forum to discuss the teaching of supervision and to promote its scholarship and research.[2] Twenty-one professors attended its first

---

1   Another such collection was compiled by Hazi and Garman in 2007 and is available on the COPIS website (https://www.copis.org).
2   Supervision has many *discourse communities* (e.g., Mette, 2019). A discourse community is a "grouping of people who share common language, norms, characteristics, patterns, or practices as a consequence of their ongoing communications and identification with each other" (Bazerman, 2009, para 1). Borg (2003) explains that in a discourse community scholars need not physically gather, but can use text (conferences, newsletters, articles, emails, etc.)

meeting in the Monteleone Hotel in New Orleans on March 15, 1975 where the agenda was to elect Ben Harris as President, to revive an ASCD Commission on Problems of Supervisors, and to include more supervision sessions at ASCD's annual conference. Its members include such notable supervision scholars as Robert Alfonso, Robert Anderson, Art Blumberg, Morris Cogan, Ray Bruce, Jerry Firth, Noreen Garman, Louise Hock, John Lovell, and Tom Sergiovanni.

In the early days, COPIS members tended to be drawn from educational administration within which supervision was considered a specialty. It met twice a year. A fall conference was hosted by a university of one of its members. A spring meeting was held in conjunction with ASCD (once called the Association for Supervision and Curriculum Development). COPIS maintained an affiliation with ASCD for many years and included the period when the *Journal of Curriculum and Supervision* became a peer-reviewed journal companion to *Educational Leadership,* which was geared more toward practitioners. Membership was by election, usually by nomination of promising students. As COPIS evolved it came to draw from the ranks of teacher educators, a group previously excluded.[3]

Today, COPIS comprises a diverse membership, as exemplified by the think piece authors. Some are new to the field of supervision; others are in mid-career; still others are now retired. Collectively, they offer a multi-faceted collage of where the field has come from, where it is, and where it might be going.

---

to pursue their goals. This is how a discourse community reproduces itself. While size is less important, stability is "with experts who perform gatekeeping roles" and novices can enter to renew the community over time (Borg, 2003, p. 3).

3   For a more detailed history see the COPIS website (https://www.copis.org). It should also be noted that another important community of supervision scholars and practitioners exists as an AERA Special Interest Group (SIG) on Supervision and Instructional Leadership. COPIS financially supported this SIG 's formation fee. The deliberations among members of this group also shape the field of supervision.

The Knowledge Territory of Supervision

As the term *field of study* connotes, discourse communities coalesce around a shared body of knowledge. The boundaries of supervision's knowledge territory, however, are blurred. As noted by Holland (2010, para 1), its "scholarship does not exist as a well-demarcated body of literature and research but can often be found within other related educational fields" including curriculum, teacher education, and professional development. Further complicating the territory are a number of factors. One is the schism between scholars who subscribe to its accountability (summative) purpose versus those who emphasize its support (formative) purpose. Another factor is that supervision "extends across the full range of a teaching career and assumes various forms to address the needs and interests of teachers" (Holland, 2010, para 1). In the name of supervision, scholars have advocated promising techniques such as action research, coaching, mentoring, professional learning communities, and reflection and inquiry. Some have characterized these techniques as "alternatives to supervision" (Sullivan & Glanz, 2002) and "add-ons" (Zepeda et al., 2020) that have each developed into a field of study, and thus, make supervision difficult to encapsulate and define. Indeed, this very diversity of thinking subsumed under the concept of "supervision" may be the field's most defining characteristic.

Certainly, over the years, scholars of supervision have engaged in a broad range of fieldwork—inquiry that excavates, collects, and examines dimensions of a field (e.g., audiences, discourses, forums, history, influences, scope, and major thinkers). Fieldwork takes many forms including essays, memoirs, research articles, and books that map the territory under study. For example, fieldwork in supervision includes the work of Bolin (1988) and Glanz (2018) who interviewed its scholars; Gordon (2019) who writes reflectively about scholars who have influenced his thinking; and Espinoza (2020) who analyzes the work of one scholar. Edited collections include Firth and Pajak (1998), Glanz and Neville (1997), and Glanz and Zepeda (2015). In their own ways, each offer a window into the field through the eyes of their authors or editors. A think piece is one form of fieldwork.

The Think Piece

Think Piece is a genre of semi-formal, professional writing intended to promote deliberation on a central concept, issue, or question. Think pieces offer ideas and points of view that are in formation for both the author and the audiences with whom they are shared. They are meant to evoke (and even provoke) conversation. Think pieces are one modality for furthering discourses within a field of study.

In this spirit, the think pieces included in this book may be useful to those studying, teaching, and working in the field of supervision. The think piece authors are not offering definitive or prescriptive answers to thorny issues that have haunted the field of supervision since its inception. Rather, they offer reflections on such issues in the hope that others will be inclined to join in thoughtful conversations about them. Our hope is that this monograph provides a window into the minds of current, past, and future scholars of instructional supervision.

Organization of this Collection

As we reviewed the think pieces, we debated whether to group them under particular issues. In the end, we decided to organize them alphabetically according to the author's name. Two considerations led to this decision. First, we did not want to interpose our conceptual schema between the author's message and the reader's direct encounter with the author's thinking. Second, even though the think pieces each have a central focus, the authors often touch upon multiple issues. Suggesting that any one think piece fits neatly into one cluster seemed rather arbitrary and only marginally useful.

That said, a number of important themes thread through the think pieces. For this reason, we have included a section titled "Afterwords," which includes reflections on the think piece collection as a whole. In addition, an index of key concepts has been included to facilitate locating related ideas. We hope these features, along with the think pieces themselves, will prove useful to those engaged in studying the field of supervision.

References

Bazerman, C. (2009, November 22). Issue brief: Discourse community theory. https://web.archive.org/web/20151117012340/http://www.ncte.org/college/briefs/dc

Bolin, F. (1988). Does a community of scholars in supervision exist? *Journal of Curriculum and Supervision, 3*(4), 296-307.

Borg, E. (2003). Discourse community. *ELT Journal, 57*(4), 398-400. https://openlab.citytech.cuny.edu/eng1121-o436-spring2021/files/2021/01/Borg-Discourse-Community.pdf

Espinoza S. (2020). To be continued: Carl Glickman's work as the beginning of the story. *Journal of Educational Supervision, 3*(2), 83-96. https://doi.org/10.31045/jes.3.2.5

Firth, G., & Pajak, E. (Eds.). (1998). *Handbook of Research on School Supervision.* MacMillan.

Garman, N.B. (2020). The dream of clinical supervision, critical perspectives on the state of supervision and our long-lived accountability nightmare. *Journal of Educational Supervision, 3*(3). https://doi.org/10.31045/jes.3.3.2

Glanz, J. (2018). Chronicling perspectives about the state of instructional supervision by eight prominent scholars of supervision. *Journal of Educational Supervision, 1*(1), 1-17. https://doi.org/10.31045/jes.1.1.1

Glanz, J., & Neville, R. (Eds.). (1997). *Educational Supervision: Perspectives, Issues, and Controversies.* Christopher-Gordon.

Glanz, J., & Zepeda, S.J. (Eds.). (2015). *Supervision: New perspectives for theory and practice.* Rowman & Littlefield.

Gordon, S. (1992). Gordon, S. (1992). Paradigms, transitions, and the new supervision. *Journal of Curriculum and Supervision, 8*(1), 62-76.

Gordon, S. (2019). Educational supervision: Reflections on its past, present, and future. *Journal of Educational Supervision, 2*(2), 27-52. https://digitalcommons.library.umaine.edu/jes/vol2/iss2/2/

Hazi, H.M., & Garman, N.B. (2007, October). Supervision as a field of study? Think pieces for an open forum at the annual meeting of the Council of Professors of Instructional Supervision. https://www.copis.org/historyarchives

Holland, P. (2010). Supervision as a field of study. In C. Kridel (Ed.), *Encyclopedia of curriculum studies: Volume 2* (p. 706). Sage. https://doi.org/10.4135/9781412958806

Mette, I. M. (2019). The state of supervision discourse communities: A call for the future of supervision to shed its mask. *Journal of Educational Supervision, 2* (2), 1-10. https://doi.org/https://doi.org/10.31045/jes.2.2.1

Pinar, W. F., Reynolds, W.M., Slattery, P., & Taubman, P.M. (1995). *Understanding curriculum.* Peter Lang.

Sullivan, S. & Glanz, J. (2000). Alternative approaches to supervision: Cases from the field. *Journal of Curriculum & Supervision 15*(3), 212-235.

Zepeda, S. J., Alkaabi, A., & Ravernier, M. (2020, January 30). Leadership and supervision. *Oxford research encyclopedia: Education.* Oxford University Press. https://doi.org/10.1093/acrefore/9780190264093.013.617

Think Pieces

Discussion Boards

INTERACTION OR REGURGITATION?

Ann Sundstrom Allen

Dr. Allen has over 30 years of experience in education. She has been teaching online since 2005. She currently serves Central State University as an adjunct in the Professional Education department teaching undergraduate courses in education. A graduate of University of Kentucky & University of Cincinnati, she holds a BA in Elementary Education, MA in Educational Administration, and a doctorate in Urban Educational Leadership. Ann has experience in K-12 education as a teacher and an administrator and in higher education as faculty, program director using online and hybrid formats, and at undergraduate, masters, and doctoral levels.

In this think piece, I examine a common practice relative to the use of discussion boards when teaching undergraduate education majors in the online format. I hope to convince you to help me discover more authentic ways of generating engagement and interaction for online students. My intent is to find ways to create a caring community of learners who connect, disagree, and discuss topics in a safe space. I purposefully did not include references to any studies or other literature in hopes of making this a practical piece that tackles my most concerning problem of practice. I use student participation in discussion boards as formative assessment of their reflective thinking practice. My hope is that this leads them to understand the role of supervision in their practice.

I began teaching online in January of 2005, at the University of Cincinnati (UC). The UC format tasked full-time tenure track faculty to design and develop their traditional face-to-face course for online delivery while facilitators (most of us were recent UC masters graduates or teaching assistants from the doctoral program) monitored cohorts. This meant that facilitators worked with the same set of masters students throughout the duration of their time in the program. We monitored discussions and graded papers. We also gave professors feedback on content, delivery modes, and assessments.

At that time, I had no clue about adult learning theory, online teaching and learning, or developing a course based on the university catalog or course descriptions. I also was naïve about the university way of working, politics of course assignments, and other functions of a department or program within the larger context of a university. I was an aspiring doctoral student with much to learn about the steps being a leap of faith from K-12 into academia.

Moving ahead to 2013, my sister-in-law began the Ohio University online nursing program for LPNs to gain their Bachelor of Nursing degree. Frustrated with meeting the expectations and attempting to find meaning in the work, she asked me to read her course discussion boards (DB) and help her get better grades. She requested I help with "these damn" discussion boards. Her feeling was that as a working mother with other responsibilities she did not have time to read all the other posts or respond in meaningful ways. After all, she had just written the same thing her peers had using different words.

What I discovered was her discussion boards were structured much like ours at UC. A prompt covering some area of the week's work was provided and engagement expectations were defined by writing an original post in reference to the week's reading assignments and a specific number of posts to a specific number of peers. What I read were 20 posts by 20 different people summarizing the reading and basically repeating the same thing over and over. The interactions were mostly agreement and resembled an "Amen Choir," more than replicating Socratic style discussion that would take place in a face-to-face class.

Fast forward to 2023, I am now teaching online at Central State University (CSU). The courses have been developed by CSU full-time faculty, and the use of discussion boards is largely unchanged since

I began online instruction in 2005. I feel as if DBs are an additional written assignment that your peers see and try to respond to, thus failing to replicate any time spent in a face-to-face setting. I try to interact each week by adding either my experience in the area or as a devil's advocate hoping to model cognitive dissonance and respectful dialogue from a differing viewpoint. I fell woefully short in stimulating dissonance or dialogue.

I sent this to students who struggle to gain full point credit on DBs and encourage them to email me asking how they can get more points:

> My purpose for discussions is to recreate the interaction and dialogue that occurs in face-to-face courses. Part of the reason I ask the question about what you prefer: small or large group discussions is that some folks in a face-to-face course never speak, but I can see their head nod, see their responses to others, and judge their level of engagement by body language. This is not an option in an online course.

> My hope is that you spend more time reading others' posts and reply to those that resonate with you. This goes beyond a simple affirmation and does not have a word count attached to it.

> Your response to the original prompt is intended to provide me with evidence that you have read/viewed and reflected upon the course materials. This does not mean write a 250-word response. It means respond in a meaningful way that includes a question or a wondering that provides your peers with an opportunity to consider an alternate viewpoint or disagree with you in a respectful way.

In response to the first week's discussion board grades being posted, I offer this as an announcement:

Tips for full point credit on Discussion Boards

Weekly requirement is your own original and 2 replies to peers' posts. This is the minimum and I do not consider this excellent. In order for me to consider your discussion board weekly participation excellent I expect the following:

Reply to others' posts the same day you post your original.
Reply to others' posts on two or more different days during the week.
Reply to others' posts include questions or probing inquiry that goes beyond affirmation or agreement.

This is an example of the online discussion board statement I include in syllabi:

Online discussions should be viewed as if you were having a discussion in class. Grading rubrics for each will be provided. To receive full points, comments must be thoughtful, responsive, respectful, and professional. Failure to post an original post in any discussion board will result in a one letter grade reduction of your final grade based on points. For example, if you have a B with 650 points, your final grade will be a C because you failed to complete one required assignment.

Students are expected to participate in discussions throughout the week and reply to those who comment in response to your original post. This practice provides evidence that you are fully engaged in the dialogue. Discussion board grades will be determined according to the depth of your personal reflection and your presentation of your perspective in response to the prompt.

Classroom discussions, online and in-person, are critically important and student active engagement in dialogue is expected and reflected in your grade. I am proposing that we discover ways to create discussion boards that are more authentic!

I tried to use discussion boards differently when I was teaching aspiring principals at Western Carolina University (WCU). I called them Weekly Wonderings after listening to a COPIS presentation by Becci Burns about her work encouraging undergraduate student teachers to wonder and reflect on their week's work. Students were much more engaged and interactive when they generated topics for discussion each week. I do not have any data to prove this, but I do want to encourage those of you who are designing online courses to examine your purpose for using discussion boards.

Weekly Wonderings in lieu of discussion boards required students to respond to each of the items found in module materials (textbook chapters, articles, videos, and/or websites) by either noting something they wanted to know more about, things that offered a new perspective or wondered how it would be used in practice. I asked that students log into the discussion board on two more occasions after their initial post to reply to others in authentic and meaningful ways.

I have listed questions that echo in my head about discussion board use. What questions have I left out? What questions best get to the cognitive purpose intended? What is the real purpose of your discussion boards?

- Is your prompt really a short, written assignment?
- What about your prompt encourages interaction?
- What is your purpose for using discussion boards?
- Are you checking for understanding or looking to see if students read the assigned material?
- Are you asking them to all answer from the same academic position or are you asking them to apply the response to their current position or understanding?
- Should we ask students to practice reflection instead of sharing summary information when they are working in discussion boards?
- Should we be designing discussion boards to be more like social media blurbs?
- Should we ask students to respond to everyone or use small groups to mix up the interactions?

I propose a pedagogical purpose be established by each person designing a discussion board expectation for students in online courses. If, like me, you hope to use discussion boards as a reflective practice tool or a direct tie to supervision, I welcome your feedback. I propose deeper examination of the phenomenon of online discussion boards. Do we want several different forms of regurgitation, or do we want authentic wondering interaction? I look forward to hearing your thoughts and suggestions.

The Evolution of the Field of Instructional Supervision

WHOM DOES IT SERVE AND HOW DOES IT FUNCTION?

Bernard Badiali

Bernard Badiali, is an emeritus professor at The Pennsylvania State University, holding a Ph.D. in Curriculum and Instruction from Penn State since 1985. During his 50-year career, he served in various roles, including High School English teacher, instructional supervisor, faculty member in two distinguished universities, Chair of the Department of Education Leadership at Miami University and Professor in Charge of Curriculum and Supervision at Penn State. Recognized for his educational contributions, he was honored as a Danforth-Johnson Scholar at Stanford University and a Leadership Associate with the Institute for Educational Inquiry affiliated with the University of Washington in Seattle. He has been the recipient of numerous awards from the American Educational Research Association, the National Association for Professional Development Schools and Alumni Associations at Brevard College and Penn State.

Instructional supervision has been the central theme for Dr. Badiali's teaching, research, and academic writing for the last

30 years, particularly in school/university partnerships. He coordinated professional development schools at Miami University and Penn State, emphasizing the dynamic environment created by such collaborations. His scholarly contributions include articles, book chapters and policy briefs. Most recently he coauthored the Nine Essentials, a description of what it means to be a professional development school. Badiali has held leadership roles in professional organizations including COPIS, AERA, NAPDS and Phi Delta Kappa. He is currently serving as Chair of the Instructional Supervision SIG of AERA and on the Board of Directors of the College of Education's Alumni Council at Penn State.

Introduction

The field of instructional supervision has undergone a remarkable evolution over the years, shaped by changing educational paradigms, technological advancements, and a growing understanding of effective teaching and learning strategies. As scholars and educators, it is crucial to reflect on the journey of this field, examining both its intended beneficiaries and the multifaceted ways in which it functions. In this think piece, we delve into the fundamental question: whom does instructional supervision serve and how does it function within the broader educational landscape?

Whom Does It Serve?

Instructional supervision is a dynamic endeavor that serves a diverse range of stakeholders. Primarily, it serves educators—teachers and instructors—who play a central role in shaping the educational experiences of learners. By providing targeted feedback, professional development, and support, instructional supervisors aid educators in refining their pedagogical approaches and adapting to evolving teaching methodologies. Moreover, instructional supervision benefits students, as improved teaching practices directly enhance the quality of learning experiences. Ultimately, instructional supervision is a service to the entire educational community, as it contributes to the betterment of teaching and learning outcomes.

Evolution of Function

The function of instructional supervision has evolved in response to changes in educational philosophies and the broader social context. Traditionally, instructional supervision was often perceived as a top-down mechanism focused on compliance and control. However, contemporary perspectives have shifted towards a more collaborative and growth-oriented model. Instructional supervisors now embrace roles as mentors, partners, and facilitators of reflective practice.

Technology has also played a pivotal role in reshaping the function of instructional supervision. Virtual observation tools, data analytics, and online communication platforms have expanded the possibilities for remote supervision and personalized feedback. This technological integration has not only improved the efficiency of the supervision process but has also made it more accessible, enabling supervisors to support educators across geographical boundaries.

Intersection with Leadership and Policy

Instructional supervision is intricately intertwined with educational leadership and policy-making. Effective supervision necessitates visionary leadership that advocates for quality teaching and fosters a culture of continuous improvement. Supervisory practices are often guided by policies that outline the expectations for teacher evaluation, professional development, and accountability. As the field has evolved, there is a growing recognition that policies should be informed by research and adapted to local contexts, rather than imposing standardized approaches.

Challenges and Future Directions

The evolution of instructional supervision has not been without challenges. Striking a balance between evaluative and developmental functions remains a delicate endeavor, as educators value constructive feedback but also fear the potential consequences of critical evaluation. Additionally, ensuring equitable access to effective supervision and addressing the varying needs of educators at different career stages require ongoing attention.

Looking ahead, the field must navigate the integration of emerging technologies, such as artificial intelligence and immersive simulations, into the supervision process. Moreover, the relationship between instructional supervision and culturally responsive pedagogy deserves deeper exploration to ensure that supervision practices are sensitive to diverse student populations.

Conclusion

In conclusion, the evolution of instructional supervision reflects a shift from a compliance-oriented approach to a more collaborative and growth-focused model. This transformation serves not only educators and students but also the broader educational community. As we reflect on the past and envision the future, it is imperative for scholars and practitioners alike to remain attuned to the changing needs of education, the influence of technology, and the essential role of leadership and policy. Instructional supervision, in its adaptive and innovative form, continues to be a cornerstone of educational improvement and a conduit for effective teaching and learning.

Personal Reflection

When I was a more active, working scholar, I would have been pleased to send the brief essay above to the COPIS community. It's well-written, isn't it? Clear, concise and on-point. Thank you, but I didn't write it. Chat GPT wrote it. Oh, what "artificial" intelligence can do—with words.

Words, words, words. Of course, words can be important as I have learned from reading much of the scholarship associated with instructional supervision. But sometimes I think that all the important words about supervision may have already been written. Who has articulated things any better than Sergiovanni and Starratt or Glickman and the Gordons or Nolan and Hoover? Is there anything new under the sun? Well, there is chat GPT. I've been wondering how supervisors and those of us who prepared them might use Chat to their advantage.

An Even More Personal Reflection

At the COPIS meeting in Augusta, I was embarrassed when Carl Glickman asked me to respond to an issue he raised with a group of graduate students. I was not listening to Carl because my head was elsewhere (still between my shoulders, but lost in reading a doctoral thesis). It's interesting what an embarrassing moment can do to the psyche. I felt bad for hours afterward. In the midst of my downward spiral, a bright and energetic meeting attendee offered a question to the more experienced (old) COPIS members in the gathering. "As a new supervisor, what is THE most important thing I need to know?" Several of us replied, but my answer was by far the least satisfying to her. I said that I could not name ONE thing, that supervision was too complex and multifaceted to narrow down to a single factor. How could I, a professor for more than 30 years, not come up with just one thing? That seems pretty lame, but I would not change my response. There is no ONE thing. But, in retrospect, I might have told her this—

The single most important thing for an instructional supervisor in education to know and do is to prioritize effective teaching and student learning above all else. It involves **several** key aspects (I'm using this clever strategy to allow a more extended answer):

Teacher Development: Invest in the growth and professional development of teachers. Understand their strengths and areas for improvement, and provide targeted support, training, and resources to help them excel in the classroom.

Curriculum Alignment: Ensure that the curriculum is aligned with educational standards and best practices. Regularly review and update curriculum materials to reflect current research and pedagogical advancements.

Data-Driven Decision-Making: Use data to inform instructional decisions. Analyze student performance data to identify areas of improvement and adjust instructional strategies accordingly.

Observation and Feedback: Conduct regular classroom observations to provide constructive feedback to teachers. This should be a collaborative process aimed at fostering continuous improvement.

Supportive Leadership: Create a positive and supportive working environment for teachers. Encourage open communication, collaboration, and a culture of innovation.

Equity and Inclusion: Promote equity and inclusion in education. Ensure that all students have access to high-quality instruction and that teachers are equipped to meet the diverse needs of their students.

Professional Learning Communities: Facilitate the formation of professional learning communities (PLCs) where teachers can collaborate, share best practices, and learn from each other.

Stay Informed: Keep up-to-date with the latest educational research, trends, and technologies. Stay informed about changes in the education landscape and adapt strategies accordingly.

Advocacy: Advocate for resources and policies that support effective teaching and learning. This includes advocating for fair funding, adequate classroom resources, and policies that prioritize educational excellence.

Flexibility: Recognize that education is a dynamic field and be willing to adapt to new challenges and opportunities as they arise.

Ultimately, the role of an instructional supervisor is to facilitate an environment where teachers can thrive and students can succeed. Prioritizing effective teaching and student learning is at the core of this mission.

What a valuable experience participating in a COPIS meeting can be! I spent a good bit of time reflecting on my abbreviated response to a colleague's very good question, when perhaps I should have said those things. I wonder how many of the points above are those with which you agree? Oh, by the way, those "aspects" are not my own, although I don't disagree with most of them. They also came from Chat GPT. The aspects listed are important though. I should have told her many of them, but, at the time, I was still reeling from being caught off guard by the incident with Carl. My feelings were overwhelming my thinking. Has that ever happened to you?

The conversations at COPIS I remember most vividly are those that provoked me intellectually but also emotionally. Jerry Starratt once said that he seriously doubted very much whether the term "supervision" would survive much longer. What? No. His statement was like an arrow to the heart. I devoted much of my academic career studying supervision.

Arthur Blumberg once told the COPIS collective that there were no "theories" in supervision. It is simply a practice, he argued. COPIS members argued back of course. Blumberg's assertion stirred a spirited conversation. Blumberg liked a row, and he got one.

Arthur Costa tried to convince us at one COPIS meeting that Cognitive Coaching was more than Clinical Supervision. Now that was a meaty, passion-filled debate. For the record, Art was right.

Ed Pajak asked the COPIS community during one meeting if teachers (educators in general) were simply narcissists in need of personal gratification from their students. Narcissists? Us? Ed's suggestion led to yet another gloves off conversation that carried over long after the meeting ended.

Lee Goldsberry—well almost everything Lee has ever said has been provocative. He's good like that. A couple of years ago, he sent out a brilliant and thoughtful piece of writing advocating the evaluation of teaching, **not** the evaluation of teachers. His open invitation to comment led to wonderful arguments about a supervisor's role in assessment and to supervision in general.

I want to note here that the COPIS provocateurs mentioned above are all men. It would be misleading to give the impression that the women in the Council had nothing to say on these matters, but that would be far from the truth. Often, women members such as Edith Grimsley (UGA), Barbara Pavan (Temple), Frances Schoonmaker (Teachers College), Noreen Garman (University of Pittsburgh), Helen Hazi (WVU), Daisy Arredondo Rucinski (Seattle University), Patricia Holland (UT Houston), Karolyn Snyder (USF), Marcia Knoll (Hunter College) and others gave substantive perspective to each and every discussion.

We could ask Chat to opine on these issues, too, but I'm afraid that we would get more of the same archival platitudes and boilerplate information. A simple truth is that supervision, like teaching, is primarily a matter of the heart, something that CHAT, and most of the non-teaching public may never grasp. Of course, it is helpful to know what great minds have thought and written about instructional supervision, but my truth is that supervision is always personal. It is a look in the eye, a tone of voice, an open dialogue, a nonthreatening set of skilled gestures and shared understandings that lead to reciprocal personal and professional growth. Real instructional supervision is rooted in the relationships that are formed from collaborative inquiry into the great mysteries of teaching and learning—and life. It is trust that we put our own personal interests and egos second to what is in the best interest of children and to a community. It is a moral activity that must consider the emotional state of each and every classroom teacher.

As a high school teacher for more than a decade and an instructional supervisor in the K-12 world for more than half that time, my respect for teachers and teaching has never wavered. Yes, there are some who underperform. For each of those, there are reasons to be uncovered and reconned with. An artful supervisor finds a way to help all teachers become better at their work. Unfortunately, administrators, and policy makers, have spent more energy on tightening the screws, rather than strengthening supports, spending more time with threats and directives than with questions or inquiries that might lead to common understandings. Teacher "accountability" is a much easier area on which to focus than teachers' professional development and personal growth. It's easier to focus on what appears to be wrong than to nourish and cultivate what is good and promising. Add position power and bureaucratic authority to the dynamics of supervision and things get even more complicated. The challenge for us who practice and teach instructional supervision is to remain human—and humane. Perhaps, that's my one most important thing. Can CHAT do that? I think not.

Returning to the central questions presented in this invitation to share my thoughts, I have to ask whether or not Instructional Supervision is actually an academic field of study at all. Certainly, it is not an academic discipline in the classical sense. How we define it may not really matter except for the demands of the institutions in which we work. As a community of scholars, we must make a case for supervision as a field to satisfy a larger academic community's idea of what constitutes a legitimate area of study. By necessity, we theorize, reconceptualize, rationalize and hypothesize in ways the academy finds compatible with other fields of study. But, at some point, our words must transfer to practice.

Supervision may be the ultimate implementation science. As such, it demands that scholars remain very close to practice and to practitioners and not get lost in the world of ideas, ideologies, and decontextualized notions of reality. In order for even the best ideas to take root in practice, a scholar of supervision must have a clear-eyed notion of what it means to be a teacher or coach, or supervisor within a school milieu. By that I mean we cannot rely solely on notions of school represented by reading other accounts, or by administering surveys, or by commando-raid research projects. Even as scholars in this field, we must stay meaningfully connected to the real world of school. Memories are not enough. Imagination is not enough. Class conversations with practitioners on a college campus are not enough. The scholarship of implementation requires close proximity. I was most fortunate to have that in a Professional Development School setting where I could be in schools every day. It is easier to profess theories, concepts, and ideas when they can be substantiated in a lived experience.

Thank you to Helen and Ian for the opportunity to share my thoughts.

Finding Space at the Edges

INVITING HYBRIDITY INTO THE STUDY OF SUPERVISION

Rebecca Buchanan

Rebecca Buchanan is an Associate Professor in Curriculum, Assessment, and Instruction at the University of Maine. She works in teacher education spaces, both preparing preservice teachers and supporting the ongoing development of practicing teachers. She examines the relationship between teacher learning and context, using non-linear and holistic frameworks to explore the development of equity-oriented teacher leaders. One area of her scholarship explores supervision and mentoring relationships in both formal and informal contexts. She has developed an ecological framework for analyzing the multi-level factors that shape supervision dynamics. More recently, she has been facilitating a group of teacher leaders and examining the ways that informal mentoring relationships, especially when they cross institutional boundaries, can provide the space and support for teachers to take risks and engage vulnerably with each other. This transformative potential of validation and critical friendship has been key to supporting the development of social justice pedagogies among these teacher leaders. Rebecca worked as an elementary school teacher in San Jose, California before going to graduate school at the University of California Santa Cruz, where she received a PhD in Education with emphases in Teacher Development and Language, Literacy, and Culture. She joined COPIS in 2018.

B y my own estimation, I'm a new scholar. I graduated with a doctorate in 2017, focused on teacher development. I didn't know the field of supervision existed. Honestly, the field of teacher development is often underrecognized and underappreciated within the broader scope of educational research, especially for those of us who work in teacher education, but do not focus our scholarship in a particular content area. I often situate my positionality in teacher education as what some derisively call "a generalist." During my doctoral studies, I examined novice teacher learning. I had explored pre-service and induction practices. I had documented mentoring and the work of "teacher supervisors." But the research I was familiar with called it mentoring or coaching, rarely supervision. The field of supervision sits at the intersection of several other scholarly arenas: educational administration, teacher education, instructional leadership, and professional development. This means the investigation of supervision crosses organizational as well as departmental boundaries. This complexity makes it a rich site for intellectual innovation. It also makes the field and the community challenging to maintain.

When I first entered this community, I wasn't sure I belonged. Historically, it appears, the work in the field of supervision has been situated within educational administration and leadership, which are not areas in which I study or teach. Luckily, I was welcomed warmly and the pioneering efforts of teacher educators before me made me feel like I had a place, even if I was unfamiliar with the intellectual terrain. I have appreciated the opportunity in COPIS to bridge the worlds of teacher and leader preparation. At my institution, like many, educational leadership and teacher education operate in different departments. Scholars in these areas publish in different journals, and despite the need (and I would argue benefit) of collaborating both practically and intellectually, institutional barriers disincentivize it. COPIS specifically and the field of supervision more generally demonstrate the possibility of considering how supervision occurs in institutional spaces (IHE's and PK-12 schools) and provide opportunities to speak across contexts. How best to support the development of teachers through instructional supervision and mentoring, whether preservice or in-service, novice or experienced, are key questions for both teacher educators and those who prepare educational leaders.

However, these questions aren't neutral. What constitutes good teaching shapes our perspectives surrounding teacher development. And the nature of good teaching is shaped by our understanding of the purposes of schools, perspectives on what students should learn, and policies that shape how that learning is assessed. The answers to these questions are value-laden and shaped by historical and institutionalized practices. Critical frameworks help reveal those underlying values by laying bare the assumptions undergirding taken-for-granted routines.

Adding a critical component into our frameworks of instructional supervision demands that we consider how power operates in schools and society to maintain hegemonic and institutionalized structures. This requires a recognition of the inherently political nature of all choices we make as educators, academics, and researchers. Accepting the position that research and/or institutional structures are neutral maintains status quo hierarchies that privilege dominant cultural norms and marginalize those from non-dominant communities. Smyth (1991) advocated for problematizing the work of teaching by utilizing a critical lens in supervision. More recent scholarship in supervision has renewed this approach by examining whiteness in teacher supervision (Lynch, 2018; Willey & Magee, 2019) and exploring the intersections of culturally responsive practices and supervision (Cotman et al., 2023; Guerra et al., 2022).

Revealing how power operates in education in order to critically examine who that power serves necessitates thoughtful examination of institutional features that maintain the status quo. One of the tools I have found productive is an ecological analysis of context (Buchanan, 2018). Ecological frameworks have allowed me to map the ways that factors carrying institutionalized norms move across contextual levels through organizational and individual practice. This has been particularly useful when combined with other theoretical lenses that seek to map power relations, such as institutional theory and post-structural frameworks. For example, my research examining the practices of teacher supervisors in preservice contexts reveals that their tendency to focus on the micro-level interactions between the preservice teacher and their PK-12 students is reinforced by observation-debrief cycle formats, which are required by teacher education programs. This means their conversations are frequently disconnected from the stated social justice goals of both supervisors and student teachers.

One of the barriers to criticality can be an overemphasis on the technical aspects of supervision. Technical rationality, and the ways that it has framed and shaped teachers' work, exists both within the field of supervision historically and more broadly in educational policy. This operates in two ways. The first is an emphasis on specific, micro-level processes, devoid of a consideration of how they exist within a broader contextual reality. This can include things like an observation-debrief cycle. These sorts of micro-level tools aren't inherently negative, but by narrowing the scope they can mask the institutional structures and societal norms that shape all kinds of aspects of practice. The second is the way that educational policy in the era of accountability has cast teachers as technicians meant to carry out work decided by others. These are related. The kinds of educational goals that became prominent in the early 2000s focused narrowly on achievement on standardized tests. In some places these test scores were tied to formal teacher evaluation mechanisms. Even when that wasn't the case, the discourse of accountability shaped a generational understanding of what constituted good teaching.

In addition and connected to a turn towards criticality, supervision scholarship could more explicitly acknowledge and unpack the perspectives on teacher learning that are either implicitly embedded in the institutional spaces where supervision scholarship occurs (IHEs and PK12 schools). While this extends beyond the work of supervision, research on teacher professional development is typically implicitly linear and causal (Opfer & Pedder, 2011). Simplistic and linear perspectives on learning are rooted in Enlightenment thinking and operate as one of the factors that maintains the status-quo in education, because it masks the complexity of learning and development processes, assuming that change is straightforward and will occur similarly across time and context. This also serves to marginalize non-dominant cultural practices around learning and development and can obscure how power dynamics nested in larger social contexts and connected to group and individual identities shape learning. Moreover, these unidirectional investigations of professional development often fail to excavate and examine underlying conceptualizations of the *process* of teacher learning and various interactions among teacher, learning activity, school environment, and other actors, such as supervisors. Holistic perspectives (such as identity theory), non-linear perspectives (such as complexity theory), and sociocultural perspectives that attend deeply to context (such as Cultural-Historical Activity Theory) present modes for considering the relationship among time, context, power, and development.

The field of instructional supervision exists as an edge community, intersecting multiple boundaries. Edge communities (Rust, 2010) are spaces ripe for innovation, because they can be nimbler and more responsive. I think the scholarly field of supervision can be reimagined as an edge community, bringing together a focus on teacher development from both preservice and in-service phases and bridging teacher education and educational leadership departments. This presents opportunities for partnerships that span institutional and chronological boundaries, considering the complexity of teacher development over time and exploring how to build models of continuous support that attend to the non-linear complexity of teacher development within inequitable and oppressive social systems. However, edge communities are also fragile, because they lack the organizational structures that maintain more traditional communities. The Council of Professors of Instructional Supervision (COPIS) can provide some of that organizational support to the field, by providing a space to bring together scholars across program areas that are regularly separated alongside practitioners who engage in the work of supporting teacher development through instructional supervision and mentoring. However, COPIS needs to attend to the complexity of border crossing intentionally and flexibly. This requires naming the barriers that exist to this kind of collaboration and designing novel forms of engagement and relational support. Moving this edge community towards its transformative potential can help foster more equitable educational spaces and support the development of teachers and students who can effectively respond to the inequities that exist within the U.S. and across the globe.

References

Cotman, A. M., Guerra, P., & Baker, A. M. (2023). Culturally responsive instructional supervision: Further analysis of a leading textbook. *Journal of Educational Supervision, 6*(1), 45.

Guerra, P. L., Baker, A. M., & Cotman, A. M. (2022). Instructional supervision: Is it culturally responsive? A textbook analysis. *Journal of Educational Supervision, 5*(1), 1-26.

Lynch, M. E. (2018). The hidden nature of whiteness in education: Creating active allies in white teachers. *Journal of Educational Supervision, 1*(1), 18-31.

Opfer, V. D., & Pedder, D. (2011). Conceptualizing teacher professional learning. *Review of educational research, 81*(3), 376-407.

Rust, F. O. C. (2010). Shaping new models for teacher education. *Teacher Education Quarterly, 37*(2), 5-18.

Smyth, J. (1991). Problematising teaching through a 'critical' approach to clinical supervision. *Curriculum Inquiry, 21*(3), 321-352.

Willey, C., & Magee, P. A. (2018). Whiteness as a barrier to becoming a culturally relevant teacher: Clinical experiences and the role of supervision. Journal of Educational Supervision, 1(2), 33-51.

Once Upon a Time There Was Supervision

Noreen B. Garman

Noreen Garman, Emerita Professor of Education, University of Pittsburgh. In addition to her work in clinical supervision, she specialized in international studies and interpretive research. She is a Fulbright Scholar who has published numerous articles and chapters in professional journals and edited books, as well as the *Handbook of Research on School Supervision* and *the Sage Encyclopedia for Curriculum Studies.*

From 1994 to 1997, Noreen Garman administered two programs in Bosnia & Herzegovina during and after the war for UNICEF and the World Bank. She worked much of that time in Bosnia with Bosnian, Serb, and Croatian educators to plan and implement an active learning project. Her other international projects include work in Australis, Korea, and Egypt.

Among Noreen Garman's honors are: The 2012 Elizabeth Hurlock Beckman Mentorship Trust Award (which included a $25,000 award); the 2009 Distinguished Achievement Award from the AERA/SIG, Supervision and Instructional Supervision; the 2007 Provost's Award for Excellence in Mentoring; the 1994 AERA Women Educators Award for Mentoring Women and for Activism in Women's Issues, and the 2004 Extra Mile Award by the Council of Graduate Students in Education.

Noreen Garman remains a member of The Professors of Curriculum (POC) and The Council of Professors of Instructional Supervision, (COPIS).

Preamble

"Once upon a time there was an old woman—blind but wise."

With these four words, Toni Morrison begins her lecture after accepting the 1993 Nobel Prize for literature. In the form of a parable, she invites the audience to consider the power of language as a force of life as well as a tool of destruction, necessary for knowledge generating.

"Once upon a time" signals the passing down to new generations; a phrase loaded with promise. Through her parable, Morrison points to generational conflict by telling a mythical narrative about an old woman who is being challenged by a group of young people questioning her wisdom. As she weaves the narrative she is emphasizing the uses of language, acknowledging that, "We do language. That may be the measure of our lives."

I remembered Toni Morrison's brilliant lecture when Helen Hazi invited COPIS members to write about their current thinking regarding the state of supervision. Now in retirement, I find myself thinking about thinking—mostly while current educational issues are making *New York Times* headlines with contentious school policies in this post-COVID era of disruptions. I'd been thinking about the educational culture wars and the place of supervision within the toxic discourses. I was discussing it with a friend one day, when she asked whether supervision was an active field of study or a function of administrative duties. It caused me to wonder whether COPIS members were still interested in why this might be a significant question again, since there have been endless COPIS debates regarding the definition of supervision over the years. Mainly, I wondered how the power of language had continued to influence supervision scholarship.

The issues seemed pervasive enough for a think piece, but I realize that, as a dotty old retiree, I run the risk of seeming self-indulgent. I should move out gracefully before my words give way to a nostalgic *deja vu*. The responsibility for the future belongs to fresh new minds committed to supervision scholarship, and I was hoping they also feel, as I do, that an academic field of study, initially, rests on the shoulders of the generational savvy of historical scholars. However, it also depends on the work of both old and new stewards of the field. Perhaps more personally—as one of the COPIS founders who studied, taught and published in the supervision of curriculum and instruction—I recognize how good my academic career has been to me. I owe the education fields my lasting stewardship. So, I'm making a bid here for current relevance.

Reminiscence

Once upon a time, in the early 1950s, I began my career as one of four high school English teachers at a small Cleveland suburb in Brooklyn, Ohio. The four of us enjoyed professional respect, institutional freedom, and curriculum and instruction independence. Each week, we would meet as a department faculty to choose textbooks, plan lessons, and decide individually how to teach (and often to complain about a cranky student or two). In this way we supervised our own "improvement of instruction." The principal appeared periodically, and with an apologetic demeanor, he would remind us about the "3 Cs" in his job. He was "checking in" to monitor our "competence" in order to assure for Brooklyn citizens'–"confidence" in the quality of their children's education. Thus, institutional "check-in supervision" was intended to oversee teacher competence with administrative confidence for Brooklyn High parents. We never considered that this independent climate was not necessarily typical of all U.S. high schools; especially such as those serving urban populations.

By the mid-1950s, the Civil Rights and Feminist movements loomed on the horizon. Brown v. Board and other contentious national issues were making headlines. But cultural injustices didn't contaminate my thinking very much since they didn't affect Brooklyn, Ohio or my teaching. I was too busy to read very many newspapers. I didn't complain, even though I was paid much less than my male colleagues, who were "heads of household." That was cultural normalcy. And four years later I was "unfortunately terminated, due to pregnancy." (No "paid leave" then.) It was simply normal educational policy.

The attitudes and values about minorities and women felt vaguely uncomfortable. But caught in prevailing taken-for-granted norms, I couldn't name the source of my discomfort. And, I was too preoccupied with the challenges of the moment, so I just went along. Even as an English teacher, I hadn't considered what Toni Morrison later said during her Nobel Lecture, "Language alone protects us from the scariness of things with no names. Language is meditation."

So, I carried my naivete with me as I moved from Ohio to high school substitute teaching in Pennsylvania, and as fate would have it, to a university career. Just two short weeks before the start of the school year, and with considerable embarrassment, I quickly got out of a contract with Canonsburg High School, so that I could accept an offer to teach and supervise teacher-candidates in The University of Pittsburgh's English Department and School of Education.

I came to the University as a novice know-it-all. I felt confident that my eight years of teaching teenagers gave me a solid knowledge-base, grounded in the "real world" of public schooling. I had come from an insider-world, where schools, as public institutions, needed to be coordinated, run smoothly, have clear communications with staff, be controllable, effective, and relatively stable. Thus, the normal routines of public schools needed to be nurtured daily—by making everyone the same, by providing, mostly through popular textbooks, the same curriculum structure with standard knowledge and instructional goals that supervisors needed to monitor. Most of all, parents needed to be assured that their children's teachers were competent professionals that knew their subjects well. I believed that education was meant to tell students what to think and to train them to become productive adults. This was my inside-world of educating children. I was comfortable there, and felt professionally successful.

Three challenging years later, with an education doctorate in hand and a title of assistant professor, I joined the faculty of the University's Department of Curriculum and Supervision. During those years of transition from teacher to professor, it became increasingly obvious that as a former public-school teacher, the dailiness of my work had served as a shelter from any significant awareness about institutional, academic, cultural, and professional dynamics of the broader cultural world. I hadn't thought much about how those dynamics related to education in general or to my practice in particular as I began to consider what it meant to be a knowledge-worker in an academic field called supervision. Even so, my worldview ideas about the field of educational supervision didn't come full on. Only slowly did I begin to learn that an academic needs to know how not to know. One of the joys of the profession is to see thoughts shed their initial fuzziness and emerge into clarity. Thinking becomes conceptual knowledge in the flow of time, discourse and awareness. Through academic challenges, this novice know-it-all had become a recovering know-it-all.

Even in my naivete, I realized that taking on a new role would be challenging. Little did I know I was entering a new conceptual world. This was more than a simple a change of jobs. It was entering what Pierre Bourdieu (1977) would call a fundamentally different *habitus*, which he explains is

> .... where socialized norms or tendencies guide behavior
> and thinking...dispositions that are both shaped by
> past events and structures, and that condition our very
> perceptions of these... Habitus is neither a result of free
> will, nor determined by structures, but created by a kind
> of interplay between the two over time, and reproduced
> unconsciously, without any deliberate pursuit of
> coherence, or any conscious concentration (pg.78).

Over time, the Department of Curriculum and Supervision became my *habitus*, a supervision community of practice, as well as a way of thinking known as *progressivism.*

I subconsciously accepted progressivism as the philosophy of school supervision. Eventually I learned that progressivism had become the natural ideology of education professors in the 20th century, closely associated with humanitarianism, shaping the language of American education. Education scholars were my guides. In their words it meant basing instruction on the needs, interests, and developmental stages of the learner; teaching students the skills they need to learn subjects, instead of giving lessons in a particular subject; promoting discovery and self-directed learning. In short, these features were advocated conceptually as "child-centered learning." Within the community of professional educators (like teachers and principals) and the academic professors who taught them for certification, progressivism provided the words used to talk about teaching and learning. Unfortunately, as

David Labaree (2004) points out, "progressivism has had an enormous impact on educational rhetoric, but very little impact on educational practice in the schools" (pgs. 130-139). He argues that instruction in American schools is overwhelmingly teacher-centered, and traditional school subjects dominate the curriculum. Teacher-talk and marketed programs and lessons are prime. Labaree admires progressivism as a humanistic mindset of the academic world, as I do. (It's difficult not to take an absolutist position when student learning is involved). However, Labaree warns against the ideological zeal of pedagogical progressivism, suggesting that there is a romantic attachment to it, and there are consequences of this attachment to American schools.

As a novice academic, my habitus thinking was heavy with the language of romanticism. Belief in individualism, self-understanding, positive reinforcement—much of it reflected the softer sounds of supervision's academic discourse and scholarship. And although I continue to have faith in the ideology today, I worry that the prime domain for scholarship may still focus exclusively on improvement of professional practice and ignore the supervision duties related to accountability. Accountability has become a major consequential concern in this 21st century hyper-complex professional and institutional world.

The Golden Age of Supervision

Meanwhile, in the mid-20th century, I joined a university department, and fate seemed to intervene once again. I was assigned an office next to Morris Cogan who had recently brought his ground breaking ideas about supervision from Harvard to the University of Pittsburgh. Morris and I were teaching supervision courses, and he shared his instructional materials with me—what would ultimately become his book *Clinical Supervision*. In rigorous exchanges, we spoke of his work as related to mine (to which he offered insightful, often painful, comments).

In naming supervision as *clinical*, Cogan was borrowing from medicine the idea of teacher education happening in the "clinic of the classroom." In this conceptual space Cogan began to situate principles of supervisory events with the intent of focusing on the improvement of teaching practice. He insisted that supervision be a collegial relationship centered on teachers' interest in student learning as well as on non-judgmental observation and inquiry as a process for both the teacher and supervisor. In-class supervision became the major structure for school supervision. "Improvement of instruction" became the definition for stipulating the primary domain of the academic field.

During this time, the School of Education's Department of Curriculum and Supervision had become independent of the Department of Educational Administration. Much of my behavior and thinking as an assistant professor were formed in the excitement of the day. Textbooks, published by outstanding national scholars, opened at least two decades of engrossing intellectual exchanges. Looking back, I see this as the golden age of supervision nurturing a vibrant field of study. In addition to doctoral programs, two research communities coalesced (COPIS and the AERA SIG on Instructional Supervision). Other hallmarks of supervision as a serious field of study were established: a journal, a task force, a handbook, and a body of literature related to significant historical events and consequential interpretations.[1] There was a special intellectualism associated with the field at that time and COPIS, along with the Department of Curriculum and Supervision, helped me to become aware of my professional habitus as a knowledge base as well as a life force.

During the 1970s, the name of my department, "curriculum and supervision," signaled a brief coupling of similar academic programs in various universities. In addition, alliances between curriculum workers and principals as supervisors were attempted in some public schools. Scholars in the field of curriculum studies also began a major reform movement, claiming independence from Bloom's taxonomy of behavioral objectives as a primary domain in the field of educational psychology. Earlier, the founding of ASCD in 1943 recognized the attempts to develop a close relationship so that supervision ensured that teachers understood the appropriate curriculum and were implementing it successfully. Supervision meant the supervision of curriculum and was the responsibility of district-level curriculum coordinators. Their knowledge of supervision was intertwined with

---

1   See Stephen Gordon's 2019 article "Educational Supervision: Reflections on It's Past, Present, and Future," which offers an excellent reminder of so many colleagues and their specific contributions to the field.

that of curriculum and instruction as a dual praxis. Sadly, over time, a growing estrangement between supervision and curriculum led to a situation in which supervisors often had limited knowledge of curriculum and focused instead on technical skills of teaching (Short, 1992). As a consequence of this "estrangement," supervision became more associated with technical, state policy requirements reflected in education administration, while curriculum studies became more theoretical in the academy. Valiant attempts to align both fields failed, becoming a sore point for public school supervision as well as university coursework, with unfortunate cultural consequences today. At this point I was fortunate to be a member of both The Council of Professors of Instructional Supervision (COPIS) and The Professors of Curriculum (POC) since I was also teaching curriculum courses.

Unfortunately, there were harbingers of the "estrangement's" consequences. Textbook authors and school administrators began to superimpose the process of clinical supervision on school needs. In doing so, they colonized the structure of clinical supervision, often weakening its underlying principles. In the late 1970s and into the 1980s, consultants like Madeline Hunter, used clinical supervision by introducing popular quasi-scientific approaches to classroom lessons (Hazi & Garman, 1988). Simplistic techniques claiming the model of clinical supervision became normative for supervisors' work with teachers, who often complained on their t-shirts with "I've Been Hunterized."

Cogan's book had become a primary canon of the field, often referenced by other supervision scholars when they conceptually named and described their forms of in-class supervision. In many academic circles, the progressive language associated with Cogan's original dialogic and reflective practice continued as the preferred process in theorizing about learning and instructional improvement. Unfortunately, technocratic commodification of Cogan's rationale often led to oppressive supervisory practices.

A few years ago, Helen Hazi and I were lamenting the waning of the golden age of supervision and the field of supervision's constant struggle for professional identity. Indeed, even the term "supervision" had become so unpalatable that many scholars and practitioners replaced it with the concept of "leadership." At the time of our conversation,

Helen and Jeffrey Glanz were working on an article. She shared her notion of supervision as "traveling incognito." "Incognito" is a grand example of Morrison's contention that language can protect us from the scariness of things with no names. It was a threshold concept that named the uneasiness I had been feeling and opened a space for pondering the use of leadership. "Ultimately," I asked myself, "is *leadership* merely a euphemism for *supervision*? And, if so, are we blinding ourselves to the consequences of pretending that leadership carries no responsibility for evaluation and accountability?" The Glanz & Hazi article (2019) provides an important historical lens through which to see the persistent schism between supervision's administrative hierarchical belief system and the progressive claims of professionalism. Both imply significant supervisor duties related to curriculum work as well as instructional-support functions.

As I think about the concept of "supervision traveling incognito," I'm brought back to Morrison's parable and the importance of deeply understanding the power of language as the significance of naming, both as a force of life, and/or as a tool of dissonance and destruction.

Language has the power to emancipate or oppress. Whether we use the language of "leadership" (or mentorship or coaching for that matter) in place of supervision, we may have turned a blind eye toward the consequences of this power dynamic by thinking that each process tacitly assumes supervisory functions, and the roles and relationships are related to the popular definition, "improvement of instruction." In this way, significant questions can be avoided; "Is supervision currently an academic field of study?" "Why is that question important? "What is the major domain of supervision if it's able to function visibly and conceptually as a body of scholarship?"

Once Upon a Time There was Supervision

In a typical academic article, there are often expectations for a final section. It is supposed to address "the so-what" of the piece, leaving the reader satisfied with well-reasoned conclusions, such as advice, new knowledge, etc., that include potential ideas about the future of supervision. For the first time in my inquiring mind, I came to this think piece with no expectation and with little hope for a good future for public school supervision. I'm struggling to avoid educational cynicism.

Re-reading Toni Morrison's lecture was another fateful moment. The parable of the Old Woman, Blind but Wise, inspired me to think about my reflections using the invitation, "once upon a time (with a nod to Sergio Leone). In Morrison's story the old woman's initial silence challenges the young people who seem to have belittled her generational wisdom by asking whether the bird they hold in their hands is alive or dead. Their naiveté falters, however, in the face of the old woman's initial silence, and ultimately, in her quiet demeanor, as she acknowledges that the bird's fate lies in their hands. Through the parable, Morrison calls attention to a lifetime's accumulation of elder wisdom and the impatience and self-assuredness of youth.

For me, the bird represents public school supervision, with educators wondering whether it is alive or dead. My remembrance about supervision is fraught with both wisdom and blindness. I think that my humanistic worldview, including progressive advocacy, was a well-represented passion (with wisdom) that embodied my teaching and writing. However, I was reminded of a friend's advice to me during the heady years when some of us joined righteous protests and marches: *"Never join a cause if you aren't fully familiar with the argument against it."* Perhaps that warning now signals the dark blindness of my earlier thinking about educational causes. At significant times I was satisfied to borrow popular criticism by progressive colleagues. We often used educational labels as a rationale for improvement without considering the shallowness of unexamined dualism. Concepts such as "accountability" and/or "oversight" for instance, became the negative language for institutional supervision. As schools face future challenges, supervision scholars may need the theories that they had formerly vilified. And they cannot totally relinquish the concept called supervision, not only because of the history and vitality of supervision's golden age, but also the legal, institutional, and professional requirements that will remain in place for public schools to be able to even exist.

The warning signs of radical consequences in today's post-COVID schools are outrageously obvious. Even as I write this, campuses are torn by protests, often leading to violence. Daily headlines warn of learning loss and chronic absenteeism among students while there are shortages of teachers and principals. Ideological battles rage over curriculum content, textbook banning, affirmative action, and social justice reform. Teachers and supervisors are caught in the eye of the storm. Schools are already being forced to address serious accountability issues and answer "who's in charge?"

It remains to be seen whether scholarship and coursework will reflect the accountability domain as the primary responsibility associated with the supervision field of study (e.g. regulation, evaluation, judgment, oversight), and also help professional educators value accountability as school oversight as well as professional growth and stewardship. Lack of attention to these issues will cause the supervision academic field to atrophy, and eventually morph exclusively into naming it leadership. In any case, the future will require scholars to be brave enough to bring the responsibilities of professional accountability into the light. And they will also need to muster the willingness to deal with uncomfortable language, reflecting the dark side of supervisory practice as well as the uplifting words of encouragement and merit.

My wish is that COPIS will continue to represent a productive discourse community and, with members of the AERA Supervision SIG, it will remain deeply humanistic while struggling with ironies and incongruities related to supervision. COPIS has an intellectual tradition, knowing that members understand each other's point of view. As an academic community doing rigorous scholarship and teaching, they represent the threshold knowledge necessary for supervisory practice.

Perhaps the most encouraging sign of hope right now is portrayed in the existence and contributions of the think pieces in this publication. As scholars doing rigorous scholarship and teaching, our efforts speak to a shared willingness to break the silence of ignorance. We demonstrate our faith in working toward supervision as a significant field of study. And to each author, it can be said with Toni Morrison's symbolic finale:

> Finally…I trust you now. I trust you with the bird that is
> not in your hands, because you have truly caught it.
> How lovely it is, this thing we have done— together.

References

Bourdieu, P. (1977). *Outline of a Theory of Practice*. Cambridge University Press.

Garman, N.& H.M. Hazi. (May, 1988). Teachers ask, "Is there life after Madeline Hunter'? *Phi Delta Kappan,* 69 (9)

Glanz, J., & Hazi, H.M. (2019). Shedding Light on the Phenomenon of Supervision Traveling Incognito: A Field's Struggles for Visibility. *Journal of Educational Supervision,* 2 (1).

Gordon, S. P. (2019). Educational Supervision: Reflections on it's past, present, and future, *Journal of Educational Supervision,* 2 (2).

Hazi, Helen & N.B. Garman. Legalizing scientism through teacher evaluation, *Journal of Personnel Evaluation in Education,* 2, (1988): 1–18.

Journal of Educational Change. 2020 Special Issue. https://link.springer.com/journal/10833/volumes-and-issues/21-1

Labaree, D. (2004). *The trouble with ed schools*. New Haven, Yale University Press.

Morrison, T. (1993). The Nobel Prize in Literature. Retrieved from https://www.nobelprize.org/prizes/literature/1993/morrison/lecture.

Ozga, J. (2020). The Politics of accountability. *Journal of Educational Change, 21, (19-35).*

Pinar, W.F. et.al: (1995). *Understanding curriculum*. New York. Peter Lang.

Seguel, M.L. (1966). *The curriculum field: It's formative years*. New York. Teachers College Press.

Short, E. (1992). Estrangement between Curriculum and Supervision: Personal Observations with Noreen Garman and Nelson Haggerson on the Current Scene. *Journal of Curriculum and Supervision,* 7 (2), 245-249.

Getting Supervision Right, Finally

IT'S REALLY VERY SIMPLE

Jeffrey Glanz

Jeffrey Glanz, Ed.D, is a Professor and Head of the M.Ed. program in Educational Leadership at Michlalah Jerusalem College, Israel. His most recently authored book, *Creating a Culture of Excellence: A School Leader's Guide to Best Practices in Teaching, Curriculum, Professional Development, Supervision, and Evaluation* was published in 2024.

His initiation to COPIS occurred when he was invited to write a chapter for the *Handbook of Research on School Supervision,* on the field's history, in which he argued that understanding the field's history was imperative for the field to progress.

Jeffrey attributes any success he has had to his foremost mentors, Dick Neville, O. L. Davis, Jr., and Helen Hazi. He has also learned much from esteemed colleagues Susan Sullivan, Sally Zepeda, and Ed Pajak. Finally, he is most appreciative of COPIS for supporting his work. He entered COPIS in the 1990s and served as Chair from 2003-2005 and 2007-2010 as Chair of the AREA-SIG – Supervision & Instructional Leadership.

He has tried to support the field with his work as Series Editor of the *Rowman & Littlefield School Leadership Series: Bridging Theory and Practice.* Finally, in 1995, he delivered a paper at COPIS entitled *"A Step Towards Enhancing the Field of Instructional Supervision: A Modest Proposal for a New Journal."* Although unrealized, he is proud of Ian Mette and colleagues for establishing the *Journal of Educational Supervision (JES)*. Jeffrey is honored to have had his manuscript published in the first volume and issue of the JES, followed by three others in the following years.

The Problem

People who haven't looked at the field historically don't understand the origins of supervision, its struggles, transformations, and single-minded purpose, which should be the main focus of current and future scholars. Much blood, sweat, and tears, figuratively speaking, were expended in the attempt to move supervision away from its bureaucratic, inspectional heritage. Over a 50-year period, supervision, as a field, emerged as a democratic, collaborative practice of working for and with teachers in helping children learn and achieve their potential.

Not understanding this history, has led to much confusion and, consequently, the field got bogged down with tangential, often unrelated social, political, cultural, even ideological issues. We don't need "to regain relevancy to education more broadly," as Mette (2023) argues in his Think Piece. We need to focus more narrowly on supervision's primary function and aim in schools. In doing so, supervision as a field and practice will matter to teachers and supervisors, and most of all to students.

Supervision study is all over the place. A perusal of articles published in the field over, at least, the last ten years indicates and epitomizes the field's lack of clarity, focus, and mission. With no common definition, without a well-thought-out and agreed-upon research agenda, and overshadowed, historically, by school administration and, more recently, instructional leadership, the field remains susceptible and thus vulnerable to various forces, ideological and otherwise, that constrain its ability to play a significant role in instructional improvement (Glanz, 2007).

Without a focus on what's most important, supervision continues to wallow in a quagmire of confusion. No wonder many scholars had and still have a difficult time defining supervision itself, and understanding its parameters as well as relevance in schools. By not focusing on supervision's essential and, to my mind, only mission, it has led many to view the field, according to Badiali (2023), as "too complex and multifaceted to narrow down to a single factor." It's no wonder the field hasn't matured and has had a difficult time attracting new scholars as well as contributing significant scholarship to the fields of educational administration and leadership in top journals.

Evidencing this persistent problem is the fact that we have kept asking, as we are doing once again through this publication, "What is supervision?!" How many times have we had similar discussions? Nothing really changes for the positive. The field becomes more muddled and confused. Such monotonous discussions rehash arguments of the past about the lack of vitality in the field, and as a result, we are left in a quandary on how to proceed.

The Solution

Supervision as a concept, practice, and field of study is simple. However, it has come to mean different things to different people (especially those with overt and hidden social agendas) without attending to its sacred mission, i.e., engaging teachers in ongoing non-judgmental conversations about teaching, learning, and content (better known as the "instructional core"). All else is peripheral, as I argued in my last published piece in the *JES* (Glanz, 2022).

Supervision theory, research, and practice should focus on the "instructional core" (City et al., 2009). Extant research indicates that reliance on the instructional core positively impacts teaching (Tekkumnu-Kisa et al., 2022). This is the important work of supervision, and it should be the field's *raison d'etre*.

The instructional core (see Figure 1 below) is "composed of the teacher and the student in the presence of the content" (City et al., p. 22). A reciprocal relationship exists between each component (i.e., between student and teacher; teacher and student, student and content, and teacher and content). The aforementioned authors explain:

Simply stated, the instructional task is the actual work that
students are asked to do in the process of instruction
–*not* (italics in original) what teachers *think* they are
asking students to do, or what the official curriculum
says . . . , but what they are *actually* doing. (p. 23)

FIGURE 1
THE INSTRUCTIONAL CORE

STUDENT

TEACHER   **CONTENT**

Learning occurs in the interaction among these three vital
components. For instance, if we match the level of content to the
student's ability level, then learning is more likely to occur. As teachers'
knowledge of the content and skills in delivering it increases, students
are more likely to learn. If students themselves are engaged in learning
(e.g., on task, challenged, monitored), then learning is more likely to
occur than without such attention to student engagement. City et al.
(2009) say it plainly, "If you are not doing one of these three things,
you are not improving instruction and learning" (p. 24).

It is important to emphasize that the structures we employ to
encourage learning (e.g., learning communities, differentiation,
grouping, supervision—especially in its traditional usage, i.e., block
scheduling, individualization, instructional prompts, professional
development, etc.) do not, by and in themselves, improve learning.
Rather, these structures must influence the instructional core for
learning to occur.

For example, if professional development is aimed at changing
teaching behavior in the classroom and appropriate follow-up is

employed to help the teacher gain a better understanding of the two other elements of the instructional core (students and content), then learning will be enhanced (Johnson & Fargo, 2010). City et al. (2009) explain:

> At their very best, when they are working well, they *create conditions* that influence what goes on inside the instructional core. The primary work of schooling occurs inside the classrooms, *not* in the organizations and institutions that surround the classroom. Schools don't improve through political and managerial incantation; they improve through the complex and demanding work of teaching and learning. (City et al., 2009, p. 25)

Reread that quotation! It's where supervision can make a difference. To rephrase their second sentence above, I'd say: "The primary work of SUPERVISION occurs inside the classroom" and that's where our field should conduct its work and research (See my new book, Glanz, 2024, which also makes this point).

More pointedly, they continue, whether we are employing supervision, professional development, or any of the other structures, activities, or processes that impact teacher behavior and student learning, four questions in the instructional process must be considered at all times:

1. How will this affect teachers' knowledge and skills?
2. How will this affect the level of content in classrooms?
3. How will this affect the role of the student in the instructional process?
4. How will this affect the relationship between [and among] the teacher, the student, and the content? (City et al., 2009, p. 27)

When teachers are observed by peers or supervisors, the observer can tell if learning occurred by examining the instructional core and asking:

1. What are the teachers doing and saying?

2. What are the students doing and saying? (in response to teacher behavior)

3. What is the task? (City et al., 2009, p. 88)

For clarity's sake, let's examine two vignettes; one in which the instructional core is not optimal, and one in which it is.

Notice in this scenario *(Vignette #1)* the advice Mr. Goldstein, the assistant principal, gives Ms. Reynolds in the post-conference after having observed her cooperative learning math lesson:

VIGNETTE #1

Mr. Goldstein: "Thank you for inviting me to observe this wonderful lesson. The students appeared on-task and you continually circulated to ensure proper adherence to effective classroom management. I noticed no fooling around during the entire lesson. Good job. How do you think the lesson went?"

Ms. Reynolds: "Yes, thanks. I thought the lesson went as planned. I wanted to build rapport among the students through cooperative learning as well as help them reinforce the mathematical concepts they learned over the past several weeks. Do you have any suggestions for me?"

Mr. Goldstein: "Well, you are a very good teacher as your organizational skills are superior. I haven't seen as good a classroom manager as you in a long time. I would, however, make a few suggestions for your consideration: (1) Instead of handing out the math papers yourself why not designate an individual from each group to do so?; (2) It's important to not only write the objective on the board, as you did, but to also indicate the math standard you are addressing; (3) In reviewing the math problems, I might suggest you call on group volunteers at random rather than go in sequential order from one end of the room to the other . . . you know, keep the kids on their toes.

Aside from the ineffective supervisory approach taken by Mr. Goldstein, he does not pay attention to the instructional core. None of his suggestions, even if Ms. Reynolds follows them, will substantively improve her teaching and better promote learning.

VIGNETTE #2

S: Hi Helen; I'm happy we have this time to discuss your lesson.

T: Yes, I am very interested in hearing your reactions and offering me some suggestions for improvement.

S: Well Helen, you do recall that when we met during the pre-conference, I asked you to identify some areas of interest that you wanted me to focus on. We agreed that I'd look at your use of questions throughout the lesson. Although we didn't use any particular format or instrument to record the questions you asked, I did have the opportunity to take pretty careful notes at various points in your lesson. Perhaps we can start at that point for our discussion?

T: Sounds fine with me

S: Great, I had some time to write out this question-answer sequence between you and a few students, why don't you take a look at it now and tell me if you feel I accurately recorded the transaction and, even more importantly, what it may mean to you about your teaching? [Supervisor shares a one-page dialogue with the teacher that also includes a make-shift seating chart with some arrows indicating who was asking the question, what the question was, who responded and to whom, and what was said.]

[A few minutes pass as the teacher reads and reflects on the data]

T: Umm . . . interesting. I notice my questions are succinct, and I think well-phrased . . . students seem to have responded.

S: Yes, your questions were well put and relevant to the lesson. Can you perhaps take a look at to whom you were speaking and describe the manner in which they responded?

T: I see I must have called on (mentions names of students).

S: Can you see anything common about their seating location?

T: Well, they are all seated near my desk . . . [Supervisor shows teacher three other illustrations of conversations with a similar pattern.] I didn't really realize I was focusing only on a handful of students [four] seated near my desk. You know, you get caught up in conveying info that sometimes you're not cognizant, you know.

S: Certainly.

T: I also noticed the arrows you drew indicate that each student responds directly back to me after my question.

S: So, what could that indicate about your teaching?

T: I control conversations by having them only talk to me? [thinks] Maybe I could encourage students to react to each other's comments as well?

S: Why would that be beneficial?

T: I'd be involving more students in the lesson . . . and, uh . . .

S: I think you're right. What do you notice about each student's response to your questions?

[Pause]

T: Well, they answer the question.

S: How?

T: Briefly, . . . quickly. [Supervisor shows the teacher the same three other illustrations of conversations with a similar pattern.] I guess they're all the same.

S: In what way?

T: Brief.

S: Yes, what could that indicate?

T: I don't give them time for elaboration? Teacher asks for a moment to think. You know, I'm a new teacher and I get nervous sometimes I won't cover my material so sometimes, I think, I look for the 'right' answer from students and want to move on with the lesson. So I don't give students perhaps enough time to absorb or elaborate, or something.

S: That's a very astute and honest assessment, especially from a new teacher. I appreciate your forthrightness.

T: Thanks.

S: Sometimes many of us, even more experienced teachers do the same thing, rush to get through, don't allow enough time for student to interact with each other and really understand the material before we go on . . . Such a teaching pattern is commonly referred to as "recitation" in which a teacher poses a question, quickly calls on a student to respond (the response is usually a few words). Then the teacher, at times, repeats the students' response and moves on to the next question and the next student. It is quite common.

T: I know.

S: Let me ask you a question, "What are other students doing during the time such recitation is going on?"

T: I guess listening?

S: Perhaps. How do you know?

T: Well, I sense it . . . ugh, perhaps next time I'd better look around and be a bit more attentive.

S: We can discuss some strategies I've used to key in on the students a bit later. But let me ask you another question, "What can tell me about the difficulty level of the content for this lesson?"

Compare the supervisor's approach in *Vignette #2* with that in *Vignette #1*. Certainly, you notice the supervisor in *Vignette #2* is not evaluative nor as prescriptive as the former supervisor, Mr. Goldstein. Although we can elaborate further on the supervisory approaches used by each supervisor, we can see that the supervisor in *Vignette #2* engaged the teacher in some reflective thinking about her lesson about key components of a particular aspect of the teaching process; i.e., her use of questions. By focusing on the instructional core, this teacher is engaging in reflective dialogue with her supervisor (or it could be with another colleague) about some very critical aspect of teaching.

The practical work of supervision should focus exclusively on the "instructional core," because supervision, as stated above, is a collaborative, non-judgmental process of working with teachers to examine teaching practices aligned with the best research in the field of teaching to promote student learning. To do so, supervisors use a variety of approaches including among others alternative non-traditional approaches to supervision such as clinical supervision, intervisitations, peer and cognitive coaching, action research, book studies, reflective journaling, lesson studies, instructional rounds, professional growth plans, etc. We need much more solid empirical research studies that demonstrate the effectiveness of these approaches.

Until now, we in the field of supervision have basically "advocated" for such efforts. Gaining a deeper understanding of the application of these approaches as well as examining the results of a teacher-supervisor process of focusing on the "instructional core" on the teacher's actual behavior after such a conference and its impact on student learning are research imperatives. We don't have much research in these areas, because the field has been "all over the place," lacking an agreed-upon research agenda. In my view, our field will not gain proper respect without the research to back up the effectiveness of supervisory practices.

I maintain that if researchers and scholars in the field focused on this more narrow research agenda supervision as a field would gain greater clarity and focus, and, thereby, greater acceptance and recognition among scholars in the larger academic fields of teaching, administration, and leadership.

The problem is that we have a lack of empirical research into the efficacy of supervision in helping teachers teach better. This is the reason that in my previous piece in the *JES* (Glanz, 2022) I argued for more empirical work in the field. It is my sense (and I am certain it can be borne out through greater scrutiny) that much of what is published in the *JES* is opinion pieces that lack the rigors of empirical research to support contentions made. I, too, in the past, am guilty of such efforts. The field, to remedy this lack of empirical work, should proactively support and sponsor greater efforts to conduct serious research on the "instructional core" and efforts by supervisors, of all sorts, who work with teachers to improve teaching.

I concluded my last published piece in the *JES* (Glanz, 2022): ". . . we need to focus our research (for ourselves and by encouraging our doctoral students) on empirical studies that more directly impact the lives of teachers teaching in the classroom." I›m all in favor of creating just, equitable, inclusive, culturally responsive learning environments. However, these issues, albeit important, should not form the core work in our field. We need to move away from ideologically (and sometimes politically driven) agenda in our vain attempt to gain legitimacy as a field to a more targeted approach that directly addresses the very purpose of supervision; i.e., working with classroom teachers to improve teaching to optimally promote learning. By answering one question, we will gain recognition as an esteemed field, attract young researchers, and make a difference in the educational community: "What effect does supervision, in its various forms, have on influencing teaching behavior that positively promotes student learning and achievement?"

By the way, Miller's (2023) recent article in the *JES* is a very good example of the kind of research we need in our field. One last caveat: I am not saying that philosophical critiques of the field, discussions, and research that are not empirical in nature, or even occasional opinion pieces shouldn't be welcomed. I am simply arguing for a main focus on solid empirical research on and into the supervisory process.

References

Badiali, B. (2023). The evolution of the field of instructional supervision: Whom does it serve and how does it function? In H. Hazi (Ed.), *Think pieces for the field: Scholars of instructional supervision think, reflect, and muse* in a collection for a session at the annual meeting of the Council of Professors of Instructional Supervision.

City, E. A., Elmore, R. F., Fiarman, S. E., & Teitel, L. (2009). *Instructional rounds in education: A network approach to improving teaching and learning.* Harvard Educational Press.

Glanz, J. (1998). Histories, antecedents, and legacies: Constructing a history of school supervision. In J. Firth & E. Pajak, (Eds.), *Handbook of research on school supervision* (pp. 39-79). Macmillan.

Glanz, J. (2007). On vulnerability and transformative leadership: An imperative for leaders of supervision. *International Journal of Leadership in Education, 10*(2), 115-135. https://drive.google.com/file/d/1o-44C4l7H7PwLCOnRM6QMDsodGJjy62l/view

Glanz, J. (2022). Personal reflections on supervision as instructional leadership: From whence it came and to where shall it go? *Journal of Educational Supervision, 4*(3). https://doi.org/10.31045/jes.4.3.5

Glanz, J. (2024). *Creating a culture of excellence: A school leader's guide to best practices in teaching, curriculum, professional development, supervision, and evaluation.* Rowman & Littlefield.

Glickman, C. D., Gordon, S. P., & Ross-Gordon, J. M. (2017). *Supervision and instructional leadership: A developmental approach* (10th ed.). Allyn & Bacon.

Mette, I. M. (2023). On divergent thinking and the future of educational supervision. In H. Hazi (Ed.), *Think pieces for the field: Scholars of instructional supervision think, reflect, and muse* in a collection for a session at the annual meeting of the Council of Professors of Instructional Supervision.

Miller, L. S. (2023). Supervision to support reflective practices. *Journal of Educational Supervision, 6* (1). https://doi.org/10.31045/jes.6.1.1

Tekkumnu-Kisa, M., Akcil-Okan, O., Kisa, Z., & Sotherland, S. (2022). Exploring science teaching in teaching as the instructional core. *Journal of Research in Science Teaching, 60*(1), 26-62.

Lunch and Reflections on Our Professional Work

Carl Glickman

Carl Glickman is Professor Emeritus of Education at the University of Georgia (UGA). He began as a Teacher Corps intern in the rural South and later was a principal of award-winning schools in New Hampshire. He joined the faculty of UGA in 1979 and founded the Georgia League of Professional Schools (a nationally validated network of K to 12 schools devoted to democratic learning of all students).

His honors have included receiving the University Professorship, the faculty career award of the University of Georgia for bringing, "stature and distinction" to its mission, and he was chosen by students as the faculty member who had "most contributed to their lives, inside and outside the classroom."

He has authored sixteen books on school leadership, supervision, democracy and the moral imperative of public education, three were outstanding books of the year by the national education library association. Recently, he co-authored books with Rebecca Burns titled The *New Leadership for Learning: Helping Teachers to Succeed* and with Ian Mette titled *The Essential Renewal of America's schools: A Leadership Guide for Democratizing Schools from the Inside Out.* He continues working with Stephen Gordon, Jovita Ross-Gordon, and Rachel Solis on the eleventh edition of their textbook *SuperVision and Instructional Leadership: A Developmental Approach.*

A delightful lunch last spring was held with a former colleague, who I hadn't seen in twenty years. The lunch gave us interesting insights and questions about educational supervision, research, and authority. After lengthy careers of clashing with each other at the University of Georgia (UGA), we had gone our separate ways to post-retirement positions at other universities.

Jim and I had been influential faculty leaders of our college representing two different perspectives on the role of university faculty with K to 12 schools and the proper conduct of educational research. My activism and scholarship, which I would call *Collaboration at all Costs*, had focused on democratic ideals of equality and participatory action research and that school practitioners had to be involved as equals in all parts of research. Jim's perspective was what I would call *Academic Elitism*, a label he would not disagree with, that only academically trained researchers should design and implement research and school practitioners and their classroom students should be subjects of study, not designers or implementers.

In our large college of over 200 faculty members, these two perspectives divided us into ideological camps. I was a spokesperson for one; he for the other. Even though we clashed and were unyielding in meetings and college-wide listserv exchanges, we were civil and enjoyed talking informally with each other.

Our lunch came about due to literally bumping into each other at a UGA occasion for retired faculty. We greeted each other warmly and arranged to meet at a quiet restaurant to talk about our lives, families, and professional work.

As we talked, I was surprised by how much his views had changed, mine not so much. Jim had been an academic research heavyweight with a record of numerous research studies with grants of millions of dollars. On his retirement from UGA, he had been offered a prestigious professorship at another university which he accepted.

He recounted to me an incident in his new position that had opened a new line of inquiry about research. He was the principal investigator with a team of research interns on a large grant about reading methods in public school classrooms. At one of their weekly research team meetings, an irate member stated that the classroom teachers in the control group were ruining their study. The member explained that the control group of teachers was changing their methods of instruction after seeing that teachers in the pilot group were gaining superior student results with the new teaching method being piloted. The control group of teachers argued with the research team that they would keep changing their methods in the best interest of their students and damn the purity of the research design.

Jim thought that these teachers had a point. He himself as a teacher would change his classroom methods if he observed better practices. He decided that from now on that it would be of utmost importance to involve teachers in the design of a study from the very beginning in order to understand their concerns and alter the research accordingly. Ever since that incident, he has written articles and essays in research journals about the needed change in researchers' elitist attitudes and the dichotomy of righteousness.

As our discussion continued, his explanation made me acknowledge that no stance taken as absolute truth about supervision, research, teaching, and learning could pass the test of time. For example, now I regret that the teachers I worked with didn't have more training in research methods in the action research studies we designed together.

Now that I approach the age of eighty and am not interested in running for U.S, president:), my concluding reflections to the next generation of professors of instructional supervision is to hold to one's moral beliefs about education and the role of supervision, and at the same time be open to understanding that opposite ideologies might have some semblance of truth as well. The polarization of ideology in our field and in our society that one side is right and the other wrong closes our minds to new and better possibilities for our profession.

Let me be clear that I am not arguing about hateful and vindictive and oppressive ideological perspectives that diminish and hurt humanity, they have absolutely no merit whatsoever. However, I am arguing that fair-minded differences in educational perspectives can move us together in respectful mind-altering reconciliations towards a Super-Vision of education for all.

Thanks for reading.

An Invitation to Think

Lee Goldsberry

 Lee Goldsberry studied supervision with Tom Sergiovanni, William D. Johnson, and Lou Rubin at The University of Illinois and taught some great students at Penn State and the University of Southern Maine. Like Dick Neville before him, Lee emphasizes the importance of supervision through direct monitoring of teaching and collaborative interpretation of observed teaching and its effects for students.

D oes it trouble you that people call themselves (and others) by names they cannot define — like *liberal,* or *conservative,* or *progressive,* or *Christian*? How about *supervisor?*

When Helen invited a "think piece," I asked myself what are the distinguishing features of a think piece. I rather quickly concluded it was writing that provoked thought in the reader. Hence, the success of this attempt is dependent upon you. What do you think? Are you truly a dependent variable. It depends, I suppose.

When we think about *supervision* in schools (whether we prefer to label it "educational supervision," "instructional supervision," or even "clinical supervision"), what are we really talking about? For some, it seems to be whatever a "supervisor" does. Because in many of our schools the supervisor is the building principal, that suggests that whatever the principal does is supervision. Well, I think that is silly. Still, maybe it explains why so many teachers report getting no feedback on their teaching performance from any other educational leader. Their supervisor may equate "supervision" with any of a myriad of legitimate duties of a principal—even though they involve no observation of teaching performance accompanied by knowledgeable feedback on that performance.

If you do not know me, I confess to being that long-time COPIS radical who suggested that actual *supervision of teaching* must include actual observation of teaching performance accompanied by knowledgeable feedback on that performance—all with the explicit intent to help the teacher recognize personal teaching strengths and potential improvements. Moreover, I have gone so far as to suggest that such assessments of teaching performance should be a collaborative effort that deliberately considers the effects of teaching performance upon students (individually as well as collectively). Radical stuff, eh?

Imagine—a school culture where teacher isolation is interrupted by sincere conversations about personal teaching practices that focused upon how students/learners/kids were influenced by those practices. Where *supervision of teaching* is itself a think piece where teachers get active and knowledgeable support in their own ongoing efforts to improve.

Remember *pedagogy?* How do we (as supervisors or teachers of supervisors) help teachers understand it, apply it, even talk about it? Remember *modeling?* How does our communication with teachers model our beliefs about good teaching? Remember a *philosophy of education* or even an *espoused platform?* How do we help our students, our colleagues, or even our own programs develop, refine, or put one into practice? If these questions do not provoke your thought, I sincerely apologize. Perhaps they are only important and challenging to me. I used to ask graduate students to tell me how "education" and "schooling" are different. How might you distinguish those concepts? Consider another concept—"college." How were the original colleges different from factories? How have recent trends diminished the work of colleges, or high schools, or middle schools, or elementary schools, or teachers, or simply thoughtfulness? How might conscientious *supervision of teaching* diminish the mindlessness of our routines and contribute to the habits of mind that characterize ongoing and deliberate educational and professional development? Think about it, please. (Remember John Dewey?)

Afterword

For me COPIS was about friends and ideas. I would list names but, at my advanced age, I would surely be embarrassed by overlooking someone. You know who you are—I hope. I suspect that you will not need my name on this to know that I wrote this.

Collegial disagreement? Oh, yes. I remember railing against the idea that COPIS should not include teacher educators because "if we admit them, they will surely take over the organization—and we want a place to focus on supervision in our k-12 schools." At first, I lost that fight... sorry, Ken.

I have learned so much from my COPIS friends—whether they were called mentors, colleagues, or students. My modest contributions have always been rewarded with thoughtful and, yes, critical conversations. I am better for them. Thank you.

Supervision for Equity: Proposal for a Third Way

Stephen P. Gordon

 Stephen P. Gordon is Distinguished Professor Emeritus of Community and Educational Leadership at Texas State University. Steve's areas of interest in teaching and research include educational supervision, professional learning, action research, and curriculum development. His most recent books are *Developing Successful Schools: A Holistic Approach* (2022) and the 11th edition of *Supervision and Instructional Leadership: A Developmental Approach* (2024) with Carl Glickman, Jovita Ross-Gordon, and Rachel Solis. Before his career in higher education, Steve was a middle school teacher and staff development consultant for the Ohio Department of Education. Early in his career in higher education, Steve served first as Co-director and later as Director of Penn State University's Office of Staff Development and School Improvement. At Texas State University, he served as Co-director and later as Director of the National Center for School Improvement. Steve completed his doctorate in supervision at the University of Georgia, where Carl Glickman served as his dissertation advisor.

Introduction

S everal years ago, I wrote an article on the preparation of culturally responsive school leaders in which I argued that neither conventional educational leadership nor critical theory is an adequate foundation for the preparation of such leaders, and I proposed a "third way" for leadership preparation (Gordon, 2012[2]; see also Peterson et al., 2013). The model that I put forward includes seven components. In this think piece I apply the "third way" to educational supervision for school and classroom equity. An underlying theme that cuts across the model's seven components is the assertion that teacher growth toward more culturally responsive and equitable teaching is more likely to come about through teacher inquiry than external critique. Teacher inquiry facilitated by the supervisor can lead teachers to change their beliefs, and continued inquiry can guide teachers to develop new, equitable practices that reflect those new beliefs. As I wrote this paper, my thoughts were focused on equity for African American, Latinx, and Native American students, but I believe the proposed model can foster equity for students who belong to other historically marginalized groups as well.

Inequity and Its Causes

The effects of inequity are deep and lasting. African American, Latinx, and Native American students score lower than Whites on standardized achievement tests; are more likely to be retained at grade level; and have higher dropout rates, lower graduation rates, lower rates of enrollment in higher education, and more unemployment and lower salaries as adults (Glickman et al., 2024; de Brey et al., 2019). Lavigne and Good (2021) sum up the problem well: "there is wide agreement that gaps appear early, persist, exist across all subject areas, and have increased as a result of COVID-19" (p. 3).

What are the causes of the problems summarized above? The situation is not the fault of marginalized students, their families, or

---

2   Many of the concepts presented in this paper originally were proposed in an article published in the *International Journal of Educational Leadership Preparation.*

their communities. One cause is deficit thinking, based on the false assumption that White, European culture is the standard and thus all other cultures are deficient. This false assumption leads many teachers to assume that students of color are less capable and less motivated, and their families are less able or willing to assist the students with their education (Castro, 2014; Kumar & Hamer, 2013). These assumptions on the part of teachers often are implicit and even unconscious but, nonetheless, such bias effects teachers' instruction and student achievement.

Cultural clashes between teachers and students of color are a major factor in inequitable teaching. A misunderstanding of a group's cultural norms can lead teachers to erroneously believe that students and their families don't value education. Cultural misunderstanding can cause teachers to misinterpret students' behaviors. It can lead to teachers' failure to engage in communication with families until a crisis occurs. Educators may misdiagnose students' underachievement that is actually due to cultural clashes as due to a disability, resulting in students' erroneous placement in special education or lower academic tracks (Glickman et al., 2024). Another cause of inequity in schools is a Eurocentric curriculum, which fails to include content related to the cultures of marginalized students. This means that the funds of knowledge students of color bring to school are irrelevant to the content they are being taught.

There are, of course, outside causes for the inequity found in our schools. These include the resegregation of public schools, inadequate funding for schools serving students of color, higher numbers of out-of-field teachers and novice teachers in such schools, and culturally biased high-stakes achievement tests. A more recent external cause of inequity involves some state legislatures banning readings and classroom discussions on the history and effects of racism, the civil rights movement, and contributions of persons of color to the nation. Clearly, education in the United States is in urgent need of reform, for the sake of Black, Latinx, and Native American students and other minoritized groups, but also for the sake of White students and the wellbeing of our society. Later in this paper I discuss an approach to supervision intended to assist such transformation.

Conventional Supervision and Inequity

Supervision scholarship on equity has been late to the table, with much of the early literature on supervision based on technical rationality, defined by Schön (1983) as "instrumental problem solving" (p. 165). Such scholarship included the application of management strategies drawn from research in business and the military to instructional supervision, with little attention to the need for ongoing reflective inquiry. This focus on the technical tends to ignore inequities built into the educational system as well as the need for supervisors and teachers to be culturally responsive.

Historically, as schools in the United States became larger, the same type of bureaucracy common to other large organizations began to take hold. Bureaucratic school systems led to a bureaucratic approach to supervision, with a focus on maintaining the status quo. More recently, state-mandated curricula, high stakes achievement tests, and externally imposed teacher evaluation systems have created roadblocks to the pursuit of equity in our schools by ignoring cultural diversity and reinforcing a bureaucratic approach to supervision. Of course, while bureaucracy contributes to the problem, it does not excuse supervisors and teachers who accept the status quo and do not work to address inequity in their schools and classrooms. We must admit that many supervisors and teachers have not recognized the need to change school cultures and classroom teaching to promote equity.

A Turn to Critical Supervision?

One question those writing these think pieces have been asked to consider is whether a turn toward critical supervision is appropriate. Critique of our educational system has helped to identify many of the problems that need to be addressed, including ignoring marginalized students' cultures, deficit thinking and its negative effects, the Eurocentric curriculum, blaming students and their families for the harm caused by the system, and discouraging families of marginalized students from participating in their children's education. However, for reasons discussed below, I do not think that the critical approach should be the primary mode of supervision or the principal path toward equity.

Freire himself (1970) argues that those situated near *both* the right and left ends of the ideological continuum tend to close themselves into "circles of certainty." Those on the far right believe the future should be the same as the present and attempt to ensure their desired future by controlling the present. Those on the far left believe they know precisely what a transformed future should look like and precisely how to reach that desired future. Santoro (2009) describes the latter type of thinking applied to education:

> This form of knowing encloses social justice pedagogy, its students, and its teachers in circles of certainty that limit possibilities, in terms of both what actions may be taken in order to work toward a more just future and what a more just future would entail. (p. 241)

Circles of certainty on the critical side can lead to judging those who do not embrace critical theory as less committed to equity, resistant to change, naive, or fragile. This type of judgment is different than the deficit thinking that comes from the right, but it is nonetheless deficit thinking. Such thinking, if directly or indirectly communicated, can lead to resentment by those judged to be deficient, decrease dialogue within an educational community, and lessen the possibility of individuals changing their beliefs. Circles of certainty can lead to doctrinairism which contradicts critical pedagogy's goals of open-mindedness, fairness, and freedom. In the words of Gur-Ze'ev (2005), "much of critical pedagogy has become dogmatic, and sometimes anti-intellectual, while on the other hand losing its relevance for the people it conceived as victims to be emancipated" (p. 10).

More broadly, Gergen (1994) describes a tendency for critical theory to distrust all "mainstream belief systems, institutions, and bodies of knowledge" (p. 69), a tendency that obfuscates critical theory's meaning and undermines its validity. Applied to educational supervision, such binary thinking can lead to rejection of theory and research from outside the critical domain, as well as dismissal of practical skills, structures, and processes outside the critical realm that can move schools, teaching, and learning toward equity and social justice.

Critiques of both conventional supervision and critical supervision may lead the reader to the question of what type of supervision the author considers a better alternative for promoting equity. The remainder of this paper seeks to answer that question.

A Third Way

The third-way model I propose has seven components: awareness, care, self-critique, expertise, relationship, community, and self-accountability. Many teachers are unaware of the hidden factors that cause inequity, even those they are responsible for, and they need to develop *awareness* of those factors before they can begin to address them. Being aware of inequity does not necessarily mean that teachers will commit to addressing the problem—they first need to develop a deep *care* for individual students who suffer from inequity. Action to address inequity requires *self-critique*: teachers need to envision what they need to be and do to foster equity in the school and beyond, compare their personal vision to their past attitudes and actions, and make an internal commitment to change.

Teachers committed to change may not possess the skills needed to bring about that change. A certain level of *expertise* is necessary to change oneself, assist others to change, and work effectively toward systems change. Building *relationships* is at the center of the movement toward equity. Teachers need to develop positive, two-way relationships with students, each other, and their students' families, as well as foster positive relationships among students, including cross-cultural relationships. Another component of the "third way" is building a school *community* that is pluralistic, democratic, and unified in its quest for social justice. The final component is *self-accountability*, including teacher self-accountability for classroom equity and collective self-accountability for schoolwide equity.

If these components are not present in a school, they are not likely to simply emerge at some point in time. Supervision can be the process that awakens the need for change and facilitates that change. Of course, we are not talking about conventional supervision here, but collegial supervision that assists teachers as they engage in reflective inquiry and professional growth across the seven components.

Inquiry Across the Seven Components

Teacher inquiry cuts across all seven of the components introduced above. In general, ongoing inquiry in pursuit of equity is necessary because none of us can predict exactly what a fully equitable world would look like or exactly how to make that world happen. More specifically, equity in school-based inquiry is necessary because each school is unique, with a unique population of students, teachers, and families and a unique culture. Like the larger society, school communities constantly are changing, requiring ongoing inquiry for school equity.

Teacher inquiry that promotes equity is characterized by expert modeling and facilitation as teachers identify growth needs, take responsibility for their own development, collaborate with colleagues, engage in ongoing improvement efforts, continuously reflect on and modify those improvement efforts, and eventually take leadership roles in the inquiry process (Riordan et al., 2019; Skerrett et al., 2018). Teacher inquiry for equity can be group or individual inquiry, but teachers engaged in individual inquiry can be part of a collaborative group with members assisting each other with and sharing results of individual efforts. Inquiry for equity can be focused on teachers, students, families, curriculum, teaching, student assessment, school culture, or school-community relations. Such inquiry can involve acquiring knowledge, changing attitudes, developing skills, making change, or assessing results. Inquiry for equity always should involve action and reflection.

Supervision has a vital role to play in inquiry for equity. The supervisor can introduce teachers to the inquiry process, help them develop inquiry skills, give teachers feedback on the inquiry process, support them when doubts or problems arise, and help them to share the results of their inquiry with others. Supervisors themselves should engage in inquiry with the goal of improving their own efforts to promote equity.

Differentiated and Developmental Supervision for Equity

Supervision for equity needs to be *differentiated* on two levels. First, growth across the seven components involves different types of teacher activities requiring different types of supervisory support. There are some long-range supervision processes (shared later in this paper) that address many or all the components, and supervisor support needs to evolve as any of those processes continue. Second, *within* any of the components, the specific improvement efforts of different teachers vary, requiring different types of support for different groups or individuals.

Supervision for equity also needs to be *developmental*. Teachers are not simply culturally competent or culturally incompetent. Rather, each teacher is situated somewhere along a continuum of cultural competence, and thus different teachers need to be provided varying levels of structure, assistance, and feedback. Glickman et al. (2024) discuss different formats for growth toward culturally responsive teaching, including introductory formats, more challenging intermediate formats, and advanced formats.

Addressing the Seven Components

Here I will address each of the seven components in more detail, suggesting some processes and activities that can promote each component. As discussed above, the suggested processes and activities emphasize supervisor-supported teacher inquiry.

Awareness

Teachers quickly become aware of "achievement gaps," but they need to better understand the reasons for those gaps. They "need to become aware of how a Eurocentric curriculum, deficit thinking, misunderstanding of different cultural norms, misinterpretation of student behaviors, different communication styles, and misdiagnosis of learning disabilities all contribute to achievement gaps (Gordon, 2012, p. 15). Readings and videos on equity can be turned into active inquiry if they are accompanied by reflective dialogue on how the knowledge shared in a reading or video reflects classroom and school reality. In like manner, presentations by expert panels shift to inquiry when teachers interact with panel members on the connections between knowledge presented and the real world of the participating teachers and their students.

Teachers can engage in equity audits, gathering and comparing disaggregated achievement, discipline, and referral data. Cross-cultural interviews with students and their families can help teachers become aware of disguised inequities and the harm those inequities cause. School-community forums can help teachers become aware of inequities in the community and how partnerships including educators and community members can address those inequities. Working with community members to map community assets can make teachers aware of resources they can draw upon in efforts to increase equity.

Care

Being aware of inequity is necessary but insufficient for moving toward more equitable classrooms and schools. Authentic care for minoritized students is essential. Here we are talking about teachers caring for students as well as teaching students to care for one another. Madhlangobe's (2009) case study found that a culturally responsive supervisor encouraged care across the school community by caring for students, their families, and teachers. The supervisor showed care for students by treating them as individuals, actively listening to them as they expressed their feelings and needs, and then attending to those feelings and needs. The supervisor cared for teachers out of genuine empathy, but also as a way of *modeling* care for others. The supervisor showed care for families by regularly providing them information needed to support their child's growth and development and by listening and responding to their concerns.

One way of promoting teacher care for historically marginalized students is to share readings and videos that tell real-life stories of inequity and equity, and the effects of both on students, followed by reflective discussions on how those stories relate to personal experiences of the teachers and their students. Individual conversations with students about their lives inside and outside of school are a simple form of inquiry aimed at increasing teacher care. Home visits are another promising activity, provided those visits include two-way dialogue between teachers and families that result in learning experiences for teachers.

A more complex type of inquiry is a teacher case study of an individual student, in which the teacher reviews the student's history at the school, shadows the student through the school day (including observing the student in other teachers' classrooms), asks the student to take photos of the student's life outside of school and discusses the photos with the student, and makes a visit to the student's home. The teacher keeps a reflective journal documenting each activity in the case study and how that activity has affected the teacher's understanding of and feelings toward the student (Glickman et al., 2024).

To show the power of care, teachers can be invited to breakfasts or lunches in which students give testimonies on the care they have been shown by specific teachers and the positive effects that teacher care has had on their learning and their lives (Madhlangobe, 2009). These testimonies can help other teachers to see the value of showing care to students and of encouraging students to care for one another.

Self-critique

Self-critique can be done on the individual or collective level. On the individual level, self-critique in the form of inquiry can help teachers to develop "the capacity to understand, challenge, and ultimately transform their own practices (Smyth, 1984, p. 426). Self-critique relates to the concept of cognitive dissonance: discovering that our actual behaviors are at odds with our ideal behaviors causes a level of discomfort that can be overcome by changing behaviors to make them consistent with our ideal selves. As Chiu and associates (2022) explain, "understanding our implicit bias can result in consciously acting in ways that align with our stated ideals" (p. 27). Such understanding is more likely to come about through self-critique than through external critique.

The types of disaggregated data described in the above discussion of awareness, provided at the individual teacher level, can be a valuable source for a teacher's self-critique. The emphasis here is on the teacher's self-understanding of the link between their behaviors and inequitable student outcomes. There are a variety of other ways that supervisors can assist teachers to engage in inquiry for the purpose of self-critique. Supervisors can help teachers develop anonymous student surveys on teacher behaviors related to equity, with the teacher reviewing and reflecting on survey results. Supervisors can work with teachers to develop nonevaluative observation tools on classroom equity, with observation data based on teacher concerns gathered by an observer chosen by the teacher and analyzed by the teacher with observer assistance.

Reflective writing can be an important part of individual self-critique. For example, in an equity-focused version of the "Left-hand Column Exercise" (Senge, 1990), a teacher divides one section of a document into a left-hand and a right-hand column. In the right-hand column, the teacher describes a conversation held with a student or group from a minoritized culture. In the left-hand column, the teacher writes what they were thinking at each point in the conversation. The teacher then reviews and reflects upon the two columns, identifying inconsistencies between what they said and what they were thinking, and summarizes those inconsistencies in the second section of the document. In the document's third section, the teacher writes about how the exercise has changed their thinking and future changes they wish to make in their thoughts and actions.

In an "Educational Plunge," described by Brown (2004), a teacher visits a cultural setting different from their own—a setting intended take the teachers beyond their comfort zone—and engages in dialogue with persons in that setting. The teacher then reflects on and writes about their personal biases the plunge revealed, emotions they experienced, and what they have learned about the need for equity and social justice. The value of reflective writing in experiences like the Left-hand Column Exercise and the Educational Plunge can be expanded by teachers joining together to share their self-critiques and plans for changing their behaviors to improve equity.

At the collective level, self-critique can take place schoolwide or among a group of teachers (grade level, content area, etc.). Disaggregated data used for awareness of inequity also can be reviewed and reflected upon as part of school or group self-critique. Schoolwide or group-wide classroom observations can identify common patterns of inequity in student grouping, teacher-student interactions, classroom discipline, student participation, or assistance provided to students. Observations of teacher-student and student-student interactions and critical incidents in common areas of the school also can provide input for critique. Analysis of observer-recorded verbal behaviors during teacher meetings focused on discussion of equity issues can contribute to collective self-critique. For example, Glickman et al. (2024) have developed an observation form and inquiry activity for critiquing group discussions on culturally responsive teaching.

Expertise

Awareness, caring, and self-critique all motivate teachers to develop the expertise necessary to promote equity. Of critical importance to teachers developing such expertise is an expert supervisor modeling cultural responsiveness. Readings, videos, and follow-up discussions about culturally responsive teaching are a start, but supervisors and teachers need to go further. Visits to schools known as models of equity are a form of inquiry allowing teachers to observe expert teaching and engage in dialogue with expert teachers and their students. Back at their own school, teachers can practice new behaviors through simulations and role plays, followed by feedback and discussion.

Clinical supervision can be used as a type of inquiry intended to assist teachers implementing new behaviors in the classroom, with the supervisor and teacher collaboratively planning an equity-focused lesson and agreeing on data the supervisor will gather during a classroom observation. Following the lesson, the supervisor and teacher review observation data, assess teacher progress, and plan future clinical inquiry. To be effective in fostering equitable teaching, clinical supervision must be provided on an iterative basis.

An alternative to clinical supervision is supervisor facilitation of peer coaching teams, with coaching cycles mirroring clinical cycles. Another strategy is to integrate peer coaching with collegial support groups, with group members assisting each other to set improvement goals; providing peer coaching to one another in clinical cycles; and using group meetings to help one another assess progress, problem solve, and adjust improvement efforts.

Relationship

As with other components, supervisor modeling is important for fostering equitable relationships within the school community. The culturally responsive supervisor *develops* positive relationships with teachers, students, and families, and *promotes* positive relationships—including intercultural relationships—among teachers, between teachers and students, between teachers and families, and among students. Madhlangobe's (2009) culturally responsive supervisor used the following strategies to develop relationships:

- Being approachable,
- Showing empathy,
- Demonstrating compassion,
- Respecting others,
- Practicing diplomacy,
- Using humor,
- Reducing others' anxiety, and
- Inspiring responsibility for and commitment to others

Equitable relationships are characterized by dialogue. In the spirit of David Bohm, "Dialogue is open to any topic, exploratory, reflective, and concerned with collective learning and shared meaning" (Gordon, 2012, p. 19). Techniques the supervisor can use to promote dialogue identified by Ryan (1999) include connecting with all members of the school community, listening to others, sharing information, and modeling dialogue. Dialogue is both an example of equitable communication and a means for developing equitable relationships.

Supervisor and teacher relationships with families of historically marginalized students are especially important and are promoted by ongoing two-way communication and mutual inquiry about how to improve equity in the school and its classrooms. This includes inviting families into the school and receiving feedback from families on what is going on in the school and its classrooms. It also is important for educators to develop relationships with diverse groups in the community the school serves and to engage in inquiry with those groups on how to improve equity in the school and outside community.

Community

The school should be a community that integrates democracy and equity, common values and cultural diversity, and freedom and responsibility. Each school is unique and continuously changing, thus achieving and maintaining such integration requires continuous inquiry and adaptation. Furman's (2004) proposal for community leadership in schools addresses this need. She would have all members of the school community participate in dialogue to share their views on social justice and reach consensus on what social justice would look like in their school. As it works toward social justice, ideas of and actions for social justice will continuously evolve to meet a continuously changing school environment. Furman suggests leadership skills necessary for facilitating ongoing dialogical inquiry, including providing forums that allow all stakeholders to be heard, listening respectfully, seeking to understand others, and communicating effectively.

To achieve equity in schools, inquiry needs to move beyond the school community to collaborative inquiry with the outside community served by the school. There are at least four levels of inquiry here:

- inviting members of the community into the school and its classrooms to assess and engage in dialogue on the level of equity they observe;

- inquiry with community members on how school resources (meeting rooms, libraries, gyms, school grounds, media services) can best be used in collaboration with the community to promote equity;

- inquiry with the community on how community agencies and institutions can provide school-based services (child care, health care, after school programs for youth, adult education, community forums) to promote equity, and

- inquiry with the community on how the school can contribute to community coalitions (e.g., for community employment, public safety, adequate housing, community health, economic revival) that promote equity.

Glickman et al. (2024) describe a community equity project in which both school and community stakeholders participate in inquiry to promote equity. The project begins with a community forum in which educators and community members select a community problem related to inequity and appoint a diverse leadership team to address the problem through inquiry. Community forums continue throughout the project to assess progress and make recommendations to the leadership team. Leadership team members complete a preparation program designed to provide them with the skills necessary to complete the project. The leadership team conducts a needs assessment to determine the depth of the problem and its root causes, and to gather information that will help it to develop an action plan. The leadership team, in consultation with attendees at the ongoing community forums, designs, implements, and assesses an action plan aimed at solving the problem. Glickman et al. advise, "The key to success is to welcome feedback from participants, maintain flexibility, and collaborate to address barriers as they arise" (p. 450). The leadership team reports results, first to a community forum and then to a wider audience.

Self-accountability

External accountability can cause some level of technical compliance to external mandates, or at least the appearance of compliance. This type of accountability is especially difficult to apply when it comes to equity. A far more powerful type of accountability is self-accountability supported by the supervisor, which is especially meaningful if it is carried out as inquiry into the progress of a change effort. As with self-critique, self-accountability can be either individual or collective.

On the individual level, self-accountability for culturally responsive teaching can take the form of reflective writing, or reflective dialogue with colleagues assisting the teacher to take responsibility for their attitudes and behaviors. A powerful tool for inquiry-based self-accountability is the teacher reviewing videos of their teaching. Teachers in collegial support groups can assist one another by viewing and discussing video clips of each other's teaching, with the emphasis on nonevaluative dialogue to assist individual self-assessment.

Individual teachers also can receive support from a collegial group as the teacher shares and analyzes a critical incident with one or more historically marginalized students, accepts responsibility for their inequitable behaviors during the critical incident, and commits to more equitable behaviors in the future. Teachers can survey students on their perceptions of the teacher's level of cultural responsiveness, accept ownership of problems discovered in survey analysis, and resolve to address those problems.

A number of practices can be used for collective accountability at the school or group level. If the supervisor and teachers previously have completed an equity audit, a new equity audit can be a vehicle for self-accountability. An equity portfolio is another form of self-accountability. One version of an annual equity portfolio has four parts. The first part includes data gathered on the current state of equity. Part two is a plan for improving equity. The third part tracks structures, processes, and activities used to implement the plan. Part four provides data on the effects of the improvement effort.

Schools can form partnerships to assist each other with self-accountability. Partner schools can send formative assessment teams to each other's campus to make observations; interview staff, students, and families; and review documents and artifacts concerning the level of equity at the host school. A visiting team shares its conclusions with the host school. This type of neutral assessment by a noncontrolling partner is likely to provide information and insights to the host school that will help the school establish self-accountability. Schools in online equity networks can share equity issues, improvement efforts, and progress with one another, and information from network members can help a school establish its own measures for self-accountability.

Supervision Processes that Can
Address Multiple Components

Thus far, in separate discussions of the seven components of the "third way," I have identified supervision processes that can support each component. There are processes that can support multiple components, especially if those processes are iterative and long-term. All the processes described below involve teacher inquiry and supervisor facilitation of that inquiry.

Peterson et al. (2013) describe problem-based learning that was developed for students in an educational leadership program but that also can be applied to school practice. Participants initiate the project by conducting an equity audit of the school's programs, staff, and support for students. Data is disaggregated by race, ethnicity, and socioeconomic status. Based on the equity audit, stakeholder input, research on best practices, and team reflection, the team develops a school improvement plan focused on equity. The plan includes objectives, professional development activities, strategies to deal with resistance, data gathering to assess progress and identify needed modifications, and ongoing self-reflection. In the world of practice, the project would continue with implementation of the plan, including ongoing assessment and periodic revision.

Action research for increased equity is another process that can be applied across multiple components of the third way. In this process, the supervisor assists teachers as they gather and analyze *preliminary data* for the purpose of identifying an inequity to be addressed. Preliminary data analysis leads to the selection of a focus area for action research. Next, the action research team gathers *target data* within the focus area to better understand the problem and to identify ideas for addressing that problem. Review of literature on the focus area also is helpful. Based on the target data and relevant literature, the team creates an action plan, including goals, improvement activities, and strategies for assessing effects of the action research. The supervisor provides ongoing support to the team as it implements the improvement plan, including helping the team navigate implementation problems that often arise. The team gathers *assessment data* during the action research to identify necessary adjustments in improvement activities and, at the conclusion of the project, to determine outcomes.

A less known process that also can be applied across all components of the third way is collaborative autobiography. According to Lapadat (2009), "In collaborative autobiography, co-researchers cycle through sequences of oral and written interaction to express, witness, understand and ultimately act on their own and others' autobiographical narratives"

(p. 458). A version of collaborative autobiography in which teachers, facilitated by a supervisor, journey through five phases of inquiry is well suited for promoting equity. Each phase includes individual reflective writing followed by a small-group meeting in which teachers share their reflections and engage in dialogue on the topic for that meeting.

In Phase 1 of collaborative autobiography for increased equity, teachers write about and reflect on their teaching situations, including their students' cultural backgrounds and educational needs. Phase 2 addresses teachers' concerns about the level of equity in their classrooms and their capacity to meet the needs of historically marginalized students. In Phase 3, teachers reflect on their past personal and professional lives and how relationships and experiences in their lives have affected their relationships with students from different cultural groups. Phase 4 consists of teachers reflecting on the first three phases of the process and envisioning a future in which their teaching becomes more culturally responsive and their classrooms more equitable. In Phase 5, teachers write about and discuss their ongoing efforts to become more culturally responsive and equitable, the effects of those efforts, and their plans for continued improvement. Throughout all phases of collaborative autobiography members of the collaborative group engage in active listening, share common experiences and feelings, offer helpful feedback, and provide emotional support to one another.

Conclusion

Conventional supervision, because of its technical rationality, bureaucratic processes, and adherence to the status quo, has not promoted equity in our schools and classrooms. Critical education theory, while it has correctly identified the presence of inequity and the negative effects of that inequity, for the most part has not been successful in assisting schools to change their cultures or teachers to become more culturally responsive. The "third way," with its seven components, is offered as an alternative to promote equity in our schools. The seven components admittedly are broad concepts, and there is no precise set of steps an individual supervisor or faculty can take to actualize these components in a particular school. The key to fostering each of the components is school-based, supervisor-facilitated teacher inquiry. Because each school has a distinct history, is made up of unique student and teacher populations and relationships, and serves a particular community, successful inquiry will vary from school to school.

Although this paper argues for school-based practitioner inquiry to actualize the seven components, formal research on equity also is needed. One promising type of formal research in this area is *inquiry on practitioner inquiry,* in which university and other researchers conduct studies on the inquiry conducted by supervisors and teachers across the seven components described above. These studies never will reveal the one true path to equity, but over time they can identify a range of promising options for increasing equity that supervisors and teachers can test out in their own schools through their own inquiry.

References

Brown, K.M. (2004). Leadership for social justice and equity: Weaving a transformative framework and pedagogy. *Educational Administration Quarterly, 40*, 77-108.

https://doi.org/10.1177/0013161X03259147

Castro, E. L. (2014). "Underprepared" and "at-risk": Disrupting deficit discourses in undergraduate STEM recruitment and retention programming. Journal of Student Affairs Research & Practice, 51, 407–419. https://doi.org/10.1515/jsarp-2014-0041

Chiu, C. L., Sayman, D., Lusk, M. E., Kressler, B., & Cote, D. (2022). "Does this mean I am a racist, distrust, or dislike people of color?" A DisCrit qualitative study of implicit bias among preservice and practicing special educators. *Issues in Teacher Education, 31*(1), 6–34.

de Brey, C, Musu, L., McFarland, J., Wilkinson-Flicker, S., Diliberti, M., Zhang, A., Branstetter, C., & Wang, X. (2019). *Status and trends in the education of racial and ethnic groups 2018.* National Center for Education Statistics. https://nces.ed.gov/pubs2019/2019038.pdf

Freire, P. (1970). *Pedagogy of the oppressed.* New York: Continuum.

Furman, G. C. (2004). The ethic of community. *Journal of Educational Administration, 42*(2), 215-235. https://doi.org/10.1108/09578230410525612

Gergen, K. J. (1994a). The limits of pure critique. In H.W. Simons & M. Billig (Eds.), *After postmodernism: Reconstructing ideology critique* (pp. 56-78). Thousand Oaks, CA: SAGE.

Glickman, C. D., Gordon, S. P., Ross-Gordon. J. M., & Solis, R. (11th ed.) (2024). *Supervision and instructional leadership: A developmental approach.* Pearson.

Gordon, S.P. (2012). Beyond convention, beyond critique: The need for a "third way" of preparing educational leaders to promote equity and social justice. *International Journal of Educational Leadership Preparation, 7*(2).

Gur-Ze'ev, I. (Ed.). (2005). *Critical theory and critical pedagogy today: Toward a new critical language in education.* University of Haifa Press.

Kumar, R., & Hamer, L. (2013). Preservice teachers' attitudes and beliefs toward student diversity and proposed instructional practices: A sequential design study. *Journal of Teacher Education, 64*(2), 162–177. https://doi.org/10.1177/0022487112466899

Lapadat, J. C. (2009). Writing our way into shared understanding: Collaborative autobiographical writing in the qualitative methods course. *Qualitative Inquiry, 15*, 955-979. https://doi.org/10.1177/1077800409334185

Lavigne, A. L., & Good, T. L. (2021). Using dyadic observation to explore equitable learning opportunities in classroom instruction. *Education Policy Analysis Archives, 29*(149), 1–14. https://orcid.org/0000-0002-2763-4551

Madhlangobe, L. (2009). *Culturally responsive leadership in a culturally and linguistically diverse school: A case study of the practices of a high school leader* [Doctoral dissertation, Texas State University]. Texas State University Digital Collections Repository. https://digital.library.txstate.edu/handle/10877/4121

Peterson, D. S., Petti, A. D., & Carlie, S. (2013, May). Preparing future school leaders to ensure racial, ethnic, linguistic, and socio-economic equity in education: The "Third Way." *Education Leadership Review* (Special Issue), 88-95. https://pdxscholar.library.pdx.edu/cgi/viewcontent.cgi?article=1001&context=edu_fac

Riordan, M., Klein, E. J., & Gaynor, C. (2019). Teaching for equity and deeper learning: How does professional learning transfer to teachers' practice and influence students' experiences? *Equity & Excellence in Education, 52*(2–3), 327–345. https://www.tandfonline.com/doi/full/10.1080/10665684.2019.1647808

Ryan, J. (1999, April). *Inclusive leadership for ethnically diverse schools: Initiating and sustaining dialogue* [Paper presentation]. American Educational Research Association, Montreal, CA.

Santoro, D. (2009). Teaching to save the world: Avoiding circles of certainty in social justice education. *Philosophy of Education,65,* 241-249.

Senge, P. (1990). *The fifth discipline: The art & practice of the learning organization.* Currency Doubleday.

Schön, D. A. (1983). *The reflective practitioner: How professionals think in action.* New York: Basic Books.

Skerrett, A., Warrington, A., & Williamson, T. (2018). Generative principles for professional learning for equity-oriented urban English teachers. *English Education, 50*(2), 116–146. https://lead.nwp.org/wp-content/uploads/2020/06/AllisonSkerrett-GenerativePrinciples.Pdf

Smyth, J. W. (1984). Toward a "critical consciousness" in the instructional supervision of experienced teachers. *Curriculum Inquiry, 14*, 425-436. https://www.tandfonline.com/loi/rcui20

Intelligent Accountability

PRINCIPLES FOR PRACTICE

Helen M. Hazi

Helen M. Hazi, Ph.D. is a second-generation scholar who studied clinical supervision at the University of Pittsburgh under Morris Cogan and Noreen Garman. In 1983 she was admitted to COPIS and co-founded with Noreen Garman the AERA Supervision and Instructional Leadership Special Interest Group (SIG) to provide a forum for presenting research related to preservice and in-service supervision. She has been a visiting scholar with the National Endowment for the Humanities and received the 2006 Distinguished Paper Award and the 2019 Distinguished Research Award from the SIG. As an officer and with a four-decade history with COPIS and the SIG, both became professional homes that supported, encouraged, and sustained her throughout her career.

Helen has been an English teacher, a curriculum specialist, a Supervisor of Curriculum and Instruction K-12, and an expert witness. She has been particularly interested in the consequences of law and critical incidents of practice in the 50 states that have consequence for teacher evaluation and supervision. Her work has been published in books and journals such as *Phi Delta Kappa*, the *Journal of Curriculum & Supervision*, *The Rural Educator*, the *Journal of Educational Supervision*, *Journal of Staff Development*, *Educational Policy Analysis Archives,* and *Teachers and Teaching: Theory and Practice*. Currently, Helen's scholarly work as a

Professor Emerita at West Virginia University has focused on the role of judgment in teacher evaluation and instructional improvement, the nature of evidence for judging performance, and principles of intelligent accountability. Her web page is at https://helenhazi.faculty.wvu.edu/hom and https://orcid.org/0000-0002-4632-0224.

This think piece asks scholars of supervision to recognize the value of intelligent accountability and principles that can guide the development of its systems. Intelligent accountability is a system of responsibilities where educators co-create and participate in a public process to account for their practice with evidence to judge it. Within this system, the responsibility of principals, supervisors, and supervision scholars is to work with stakeholders to develop, facilitate, and monitor a system to ensure its success.[3] In addition, supervisors could share their own accounting system with teachers as an example. Supervision scholars can promote, study, and explicate concepts that can enrich its evolving discourse.

The Crisis of Mistrust

O'Neill (2002) believes that we are in a crisis of mistrust of officials and institutions, especially schools. This crisis appears familiar and perhaps is seeded by the crisis of confidence in the professions and professional knowledge that Schon (1983) wrote about as did others who followed (e.g., Nichols, 2017; Oreskes, 2019; Schwartz & Sharpe, 2010). The public expects to trust the water they drink, the food they eat, and the medicine they take. Historically, the public has relied on professionals to follow codes of conduct and comply with regulations. For those with neither, there is still an expectation to do what is right or moral. Trust is social capital that depends on the good will of many yet can be easily betrayed.

---

3   Supervisors might be tempted to provide oversight. However, when someone other than the teacher provides oversight, then accountability, knowledge generation, and expertise become external to the teacher. This takes away teacher agency and responsibility as well as reinforces hegemonic relationships. It also forces competition among teachers rather than collaboration and mutual learning.

Institutions in the U.S. have developed sophisticated ways to address mistrust.[4] In education, it has taken many forms to include new standards, legislation and regulation with sanctions, memoranda and guidance, targeted funding, and ever-increasing surveillance. Today policymakers return to school takeovers,[5] and continue to use tests scores to evaluate teachers and to justify professional development expenditures, while educators try to sell "what works," "best practice," "research-based," and "scaling-up" remedies, amidst complex and idiosyncratic teachers, learners, and classrooms where there is uncertainty in many actions. While the intent is better performance of teachers and students, "beneath this admirable rhetoric the real focus is on performance indicators chosen for ease of measure and control rather than because they measure quality of performance accurately" (O'Neill, 2002, p. 54). Many existing accountability schemes undermine professional judgment, result in more detailed centralized control, and promote "a culture of suspicion, low morale, and may ultimately lead to professional cynicism" (O'Neill, 2002, p. 57).

Onora O'Neill (2013) charges these approaches with "malpractice" and "educational vandalism" for the "perverse effects" that result. Others call this dysfunction the "terrors of performative accountability" (e.g., Ball, 2003; Holloway & Brass, 2018; Muller, 2019). Despite these problems, accountability remains important to institutions, individuals, and the public. It serves the public interest where students, parents and taxpayers are the clients, stakeholders, and consumers of education (Alkin & Christie, 2004). In her critique of school reform, Nell Noddings (2007) reminds us that the practice of accountability was borrowed from business. When applied to education, educators may have overlooked that accountability requires educators to be responsible. She reminds us that teachers are and have been responsible for their students' learning in general. Only recently has this accountability included detailed specific outcomes and levels of performance on standards which are not easily measured.

---

4   See Lillejord (2020) for a fuller description and explanation of accountability in the U.S. as well as international settings.

5   For example, the Houston Texas School District may be a harbinger of more school takeovers to include a return to merit pay, district-supplied lesson plans, cameras in classrooms to surveil disruptive students, and libraries now called team centers where disruptive students go (Blad, 2023).

In response to this crisis of mistrust, O'Neill (2002, p. 58) calls for educators to engage in *intelligent accountability*: to "give an *account* of what they have done, and of their successes or failures to others who have sufficient time and experience to assess the evidence and report on it." Rather than using the noun "accountability" which has become problematic, especially when connoting blame "answerability, blameworthiness, liability, and the expectation of account-giving" ("Accountability," *The Free Dictionary*, 2023, para 1)—supervisors should consider the verb "to account" which can mean "to give an explanation" ("To account v.1.12.," *The Free Dictionary*, 2023). This approach appears consistent with Scriven's (1994) view of accountability where "accountability obliges you to be able to demonstrate that success to third parties....and hence that you are in fact successful" (p. 159).[6] Furthermore, as Bevir (2009, "Accountability: Definition") contends, teachers are civil servants or governmental employees paid by taxpayers:

> [W]hen people are meant to pursue the will and/or interests of others, they give an account of their actions to those others who are then able to decide whether to reward or censure them for the actions. Accountability thus conveys the idea that an agent (such as an elected politician or a civil servant) is responsible for acting on behalf of a principal (such as a citizen or government minister, respectively) to whom they should respond and report. The principal is thereby able to hold the agent accountable for his or her actions.

Didau (2020) argues, as does O'Neill, that the current accountability climate is a deficit model that restricts rather than motivates or supports teachers. "In a deficit model, poor performance is seen as an error or malfunction, as something requiring blame and correction" (Didau, 2020, p. 79).[7] In contrast, he says that an intelligent accountability

---

6 Elsewhere I have argued that in their work with teachers, principals should not be "delivering feedback" and that supervisors should help teachers to collect evidence in order to self-evaluate (Hazi, 2024, forthcoming).
7 Ironically mistakes are not tolerated yet can contribute to learning. When students get feedback about mistakes, they "feel disappointed in themselves or embarrassed. They also

system requires the judicious balancing of trust and a surplus approach to accountability.

Teacher evaluation has become dysfunctional and should be not viewed as an accountability system. One of its many problems is that teachers have limited say in evidence selection. Teachers are accustomed to administrators presenting them with standardized test scores and ratings on an evaluation rubric, rather than participating in evidence selection.[8] Both tend to be out of context and unrelated to a lesson, subject, grade level, and student ability.[9] Decontextualized evidence minimizes its usefulness. Supervisors should consider situating evidence in its many contexts and help teachers to individualize their collection of evidence.

Principles of a System for Intelligent Accountability

There are several principles that form the foundation of an intelligent accountability system. This section uses the writings of O'Neill (2002, 2013), Didau (2020), and others[10] to formulate principles to guide the development of a system for educators with a focus on teachers.

Participation is voluntary. When teachers have the option to decide about their participation in a process, they are treated as professionals (Hargreaves, 1994). Then there is no need for leaders to be concerned about motivating teacher buy-in or ownership. Instead, teachers come willingly. If they discover in their participation, that their willingness changes due to time, expectations, or benefits, then teachers should be able to withdraw. Forced participation only creates tensions, mistrust, and contrived relationships.

Participants co-create its design. When individuals have a say in creating a process of accountability, they are able to identify benefits and flaws, and to bring perspectives and solutions that might otherwise

---

quickly learn that mistakes are bad and should be avoided, because … they've lost points with each mistake" (Mangels, 2023, p. 3). At Corbett Prep, an independent day school in Tampa, FL students and teachers operate in a culture where mistakes mean learning (Hazi, 2023).

8   See Hazi (2022) for more detailed explanations of the dysfunctional nature of teacher evaluation.

9   Standardized test scores have been weaponized against teachers (Hening, 2021). Such tests are presented as numbers that are difficult to understand and fail to indicate what teachers should do to improve (Ebbeler et al., 2017).

10 See for example the special issue of the *Journal of Educational Change* Volume 21 (2020).

not be known or considered (Behrstock-Sherratt et al., 2013). Most importantly, they can ensure that its results are useful. In education, teachers, leaders, students, parents, and taxpayers are all stakeholders in such a system. Their participation involves negotiations so that the result is useful and that the process balances potentially competing interests.

An accountability system has self-evaluation. Self-evaluation has long been addressed in the writings of teacher evaluation but considered a method fraught with problems. Only recently has it been reconsidered as a professional development strategy (Stronge & Tucker, 2003). It is "a process in which teachers make judgments about the adequacy and effectiveness of their own knowledge, performance, beliefs, and effects for the purpose of self-improvement" (Airasian & Gullickson, 2006, p. 186). What is missing from past and current conceptualizations is that teachers should share their self-evaluations in public.

The system establishes and supports a community. As noted by Scriven (1994), accounting should be done to a third party. Instead of isolation and individualism, teachers can participate in and are first accountable to a community of like-minded peers (Hargreaves, 1994). Teachers have a responsibility to support and help each other collect, share, and publicly reflect on evidence. This public sharing is not a confessional of incompetence, but a safe space where teachers can disclose what troubles them about a student, group, technique, or process and provide another set of eyes to understand and act upon it.

Interpretation of evidence is shaped by many factors including individual beliefs, experience, and knowledge. Since people tend to notice data that support their beliefs and experiences, and ignore that which contradicts, communal sharing allows others to confirm or challenge the evidence presented and extend and deepen the teacher's thinking and future goal setting.

Self-evaluation is evidence-informed, i.e., one where "there is some evidence that educators should take into consideration" but is "more suggestive than definitive" (Hess, 2023, para 2-5).[11] Therefore evidence is helpful to interpreting a teacher's impact, but not conclusive.

---

11 Hess (2023) describes the limitations of using the term "research-based" in the same way medicine uses it. While the U.S. Department of Education and the Institute of Education Sciences have tried to elevate the use of research in educational decision making through law

One dysfunctional aspect of accountability systems has been that evidence is too narrowly conceived, is not always understood, and does not reflect what students have been taught (Datnow, 2020). Teachers also complain that large-scale standardized test score data do not help them improve and are privileged above other evidence.

Evidence literacy is important. There are multiple forms of evidence that can be used to judge teaching. They include: the teacher's own self-evaluation and reflections, interviews and surveys of students, student learning on and engagement with tasks, peer observations, and results of formative assessments. However, some teachers find feedback from leader walkthroughs to be less helpful (e.g., Mockler & Stacey, 2021).

Evaluation by rubric tells teachers about their actions and behaviors while teaching, but rarely provides evidence. While helpful when positive, Guskey and Link (2022) found that teachers especially wanted to know about their students' learning so that they could plan for corrective instruction. To evaluate the success of a lesson or unit, teachers might ask: "Have I accomplished my lesson's objectives?" or "How will I know this lesson is successful?" The teacher can select evidence that might include: the lesson plan with student answers to questions, analysis of homework or teacher made tests, or a focus on on-task behaviors or errors. Such evidence can be recorded on a seating chart or room diagram, and in some instances by video. This then allows the teacher to use the evidence to make decisions to reteach or move on.

Evidence can also address the questions: "What makes my practice successful?" and "What progress have I made?" In these questions, the teacher shares information about the process of how the evidence was used, how one's practice (thinking and/or behavior) improved for the better, and what are the next goals or steps that teacher may take. With evidence literacy, teachers can then begin to evaluate their practice so that they are accountable to themselves, their students, their colleagues, and the public.

---

and the What Works Clearing House, many studies cannot be replicated and "few educational interventions are understood or implemented that precisely" (para 2).

Hunches for Temporary Closure

While I am just beginning to explicate a system for intelligent accountability, I have come to "intuitive hunches" that may later evolve into principles, pre-requisites, or assumptions. The first is that intelligent accountability is a system for professional development with a focus on authentic teacher learning. I could be tempted to brand this system as one for teacher evaluation. However, teacher evaluation is more concerned about changing teacher behaviors and less about their learning. Teacher evaluation also has so many regulations and legal mandates that make it dysfunctional and resistant to fixing.

Intelligent accountability supplements—but does not supplant—a teacher evaluation system. In teacher evaluation, a principal's duty is to ensure that teachers "do no harm." Akin to the physicians' Hippocratic Oath, the principle of doing no harm seems applicable in educational practice. Principals and supervisors may be in a position to notice teachers, whose actions (e.g., corporal punishment, sexual abuse, bullying, exposure to unsafe, unsanitary, or toxic conditions) may by omission or commission, subject students to harm. In such cases, principals have a duty to act which may be to notify, investigate, correct, or dismiss.

Can teacher evaluation be expected to improve teaching? Perhaps not. Not all principals or supervisors may be able to provide instructional improvement, a responsibility fraught with complexity and ambiguity, and that requires will, skill, and time from principals as well as teachers. There is still much to learn about why and how teachers change their practice over time. We know that most teachers want their students to learn, but there is much uncertainty about the abilities and conditions that promote and hinder learning.

Principles of intelligent accountability seem consistent with the rationale for clinical supervision and some of its concepts: self-knowledge, uncertainty, teacher involvement, colleagueship, and a stable data base. For example, self-knowledge about how one notices, distorts, or overlooks information is important to address when making judgments and regulating one's own behavior. Clinical supervision helps the teacher "gain new and more reliable knowledge about himself [sic] as a teacher… and helps him persevere in efforts to improve his teaching" (Cogan, 1973, p. 72). Another example is colleagueship that is "at the heart of clinical supervision," a working relationship that enables the teacher to share equally in its design and in the changes to be made (Cogan, 1973, p. 58). But the teacher and supervisor relationship is complicated. It may be difficult, if supervisors are responsible for evaluation, or if they differ in how each sees the presence or absence of a pattern or the results of teaching. In addition, teachers may say they want supervision, yet fail to give supervisors access to their thinking and teaching vulnerabilities.

Finally, interested supervision scholars can conduct research that can aid in explicating concepts relevant to the kind of intelligent accountability proposed herein. They include, but are not limited, to noticing, situated evidence, evidence literacy, an evaluative mindset, the power of corroboration, and how peer observation can support teacher learning.

References

Alkin, M., & Christie, C. (2004). An evaluation theory tree. In M. Alkin (Ed.) *Evaluation roots: Tracing theorists' views and influences* (pp. 12-65). Sage.

Airasian, P. & Gullickson, A. (2006). Teacher self-evaluation. In J. Stronge (Ed.), *Evaluating teaching: A guide to current thinking and best practice* (2nd ed.) (pp.186-211). Corwin Press.

Ball, S. (2003). The teacher's soul and the terror of performativity. *Journal of Education Policy, 18(*2), 215-228. https://doi.org/10.1080/0268093022000043065

Behrstock-Sherratt, E., Rizzolo, A., Laine, S., & Friedman, W. (2013). *Everyone at the table: Engaging teachers in evaluation reform.* Jossey-Bass.

Bevir, M. (2009). Accountability: Definition. *Key concepts in governance.* https://search.credoreference.com/articles/Qm9va0FydGljbGGU6OTM4NDI2

Blad, E. (2023, September 1). Houston's sweeping school changes: Will they be a case study—or cautionary tale? *Education Week.* https://www.edweek.org/leadership/houstons-sweeping-school-changes-will-they-be-a-case-study-or-cautionary-tale/2023/09?utm_source=nl&utm_medium=eml&utm_campaign=eu&M=7638039&UUID=5db99379423bd8f2b72457b68b37431b&T=10171824

De Vynck, G. (2023, August 29). AI images are getting harder to spot. Google thinks it has a solution. *The Washington Post.* https://www.washingtonpost.com/technology/2023/08/29/google-wants-watermark-ai-generated-images-stop-deepfakes/?utm_campaign=wp_post_most&utm_medium=email&utm_source=newsletter&wpisrc=nl_most

Datnow, A. (2020). The role of teachers in educational reform: A 20-year perspective. *Journal of Educational Change, 21*, 431-441. https://doi.org/10.1007/s10833-020-09372-5

Didau, D. (2020). *Intelligent accountability: Creating the conditions for teachers to thrive.* John Catt.

Ebbeler, J., Poortman, C., Schildkamp, K., & Pieters, J. (2017). The effects of a data use intervention on educators' satisfaction and data literacy. *Educational Assessment, Evaluation Accountability, 29*, 83-105. https://doi.org/10.1007/s11092-016-9251-z

The Free Dictionary. (2023). To account. https://www.thefreedictionary.com/To+account

Guskey, T., & Link, L. (2022, Winter). Feedback for teachers: What evidence do teachers find most useful? *AASA Journal of Scholarship and Practice*, 18(4), 9-20. https://www.aasa.org/docs/default-source/publications/journal-of-scholarship-and-practice/jsp-winter2022-final-v4.pdf?sfvrsn=e1762872_4

Hargreaves, D. (1994). The new professionalism: The synthesis of professional and institutional development. *Teaching and Teacher Education, 10*(4), 423-438. https://doi.org/10.1016/0742-051X(94)90023-X

Hazi, H. M. (2022). Rethinking the dual purposes of teacher evaluation. *Teachers and Teaching: Theory and Practice.* https://doi.org/10.1080/13540602.2022.2103533

Hazi, H. M. (2023). (Re)imagined teacher learning and improvement with systems thinking: The case of Corbett Preparatory School at I. D. S. In K. M. Snyder & K. J. Snyder (Eds.), *Regenerating schools as living systems: Success stories of systems thinking in action.* Rowman & Littlefield.

Hazi, H. M. (2024). The trouble with 'delivering feedback: reflections of a supervision scholar. *Journal of Educational Supervision, 7*(1), 85-103. https://doi.org/10.31045/jes.7.1.5

Hazi, H. M. (forthcoming). Rethink teacher evaluation as professional development. In I. Mette, D. Cormier & Y. Oliveras-Ortiz (Eds.) *Culturally responsive instructional supervision.* Teachers College Press.

Henig, J. (2021, February 9). 'Data' has become a dirty word to public education advocates. It doesn't have to be. *Education Week.* https://www.edweek.org/policy-politics/opinion-data-has-become-a-dirty-word-to-public-education-advocates-it-doesnt-have-to-be/2021/02

Hess, R. (2023, April 18). The promises and limits of 'evidence-based practice.' *Education Week.* https://www.edweek.org/teaching-learning/opinion-the-promises-and-limits-of-evidence-based-practice/2023/04

Holloway, J., & Brass, J. (2018). Making accountable teachers: The terrors and pleasures of performativity. *Journal of Education Policy, 33*(3), 361-382. https://doi.org/10.1080/02680939.2017.1372636

Lillejord, S. (2020). From 'unintelligent' to intelligent accountability. *Journal of Educational Change, 21*, 1-18. https://doi.org/10.1007/s10833-020-09379-y

Mangels, J. (2023, August 23). Don't erase that mistake. *ASCD: Blogs* https://www.ascd.org/blogs/dont-erase-that-mistake

Mockler, N., & Stacey, M. (2021). Evidence of teaching practice in an age of accountability: When what can be counted isn't all that counts. *Oxford Review of Education, 47*(2), 170-188. https://doi.org/10.1080/03054985.2020.1822794

Muller, J. (2019). *The tyranny of metrics*. Princeton University Press.

Nichols, T. (2017). *The death of expertise: The campaign against established knowledge and why it matters*. Oxford University Press.

Noddings, N. (2007). When school reform goes wrong. Teachers College Press.

O'Neill, O. (2002). *A question of trust: The BBC Reith lectures 2002*. Cambridge University Press.

O'Neill, O. (2013). Intelligent accountability in education, *Oxford Review of Education, 39*(1), 4-16. https://doi.org/10.1080/03054985.2013.764761

Oreskes, N. (2019). *Why trust science?* Princeton University Press.

Schon, D. (1983). *The reflective practitioner: How professionals think in action*. New York: Basic Books, Inc.

Schwartz, b., & Sharpe K. (2010). *Practical wisdom: The right way to do the right thing*. Penguin Group.

Scriven, M. (1994). Duties of a teacher. *Journal of Personnel Evaluation in Education, 8*(2), 151-184. https://doi.org/10.1007/BF00972261

Stronge, J., & Tucker, P. (2003). *Handbook on teacher evaluation: Assessing and improving performance*. Eye on Education.

Tan, R., & Cabato, R. (2023, August 23). Behind the AI boom, an army of overseas workers in 'digital sweatshops.' *The Washington Post*. https://www.washingtonpost.com/world/2023/08/28/scale-ai-remotasks-philippines-artificial-intelligence/?utm_campaign=wp_post_most&utm_medium=email&utm_source=newsletter&wpisrc=nl_most

Reflection of the Field of Instructional Supervision

Qunisha Johnson

Dr. Qunisha Johnson is a true Texas scholar, with a Bachelor of Arts degree in psychology from the University of Texas in Austin, a Master of Arts in professional counseling from Texas State University, and a Doctorate of Education focused on educational leadership from Tarleton State University. She has an extensive background in education, with 15 years of experience, including 10 years as a school counselor for grades K-12. Presently, she serves as the associate principal of J.H. Hines Elementary School in Waco, TX. Her current school has several new teachers and serves a 100% low socio-economic population of students. Driven by her passion for creating comprehensive social and emotional learning (SEL) programs, she has spearheaded diversity, equity, and inclusion initiatives across multiple schools. She has also worked with her campuses to assist in equipping pre-service teachers with understanding theory versus practice. She was the recipient of the 2023 Blumberg/Pajak Scholar award for her research on retaining teachers of color, under the supervision of Dr. Don Beach. Dr. Johnson leads with the belief that everyone can overcome obstacles, shatter ceilings, and build bridges so people can elevate people.

W hen I was a school counselor, I offered space for new teachers to understand differences between the theory they were taught and the reality of the trenches where they worked. Now as a campus administrator, supervising new and veteran teachers, I find that instructional supervision must change because the nature of education is changing. I had hopes that supervision could be used to develop best practices in those new to a field. However, I have found that although this is my altruistic hope for supervision, it is not always the outcome. The wrong approach to supervision can cause new teachers to turn away from the profession despite their potential.

I recall a new teacher who needed support emotionally and pedagogically and struggled with the idea of leaving the profession because of the lack of support, only to see her as an individual who just may not follow a specific script. The field of instructional supervision has come to a point where it may need to consider being as flexible as the field that its students enter: Education.

The field of instructional supervision should serve adult students. The outcomes of good supervision will benefit the children in any educational sector. Instructional supervision requires understanding how children learn and how adults change and instill good habits. As a counselor for most of my career, I have watched how the greatest need in supervision is an understanding of the stressors of the profession.

Instructional supervision has a duty to stay on top of the current "state" of instructional practices and the "state" of students entering the classroom. It is difficult to stay relevant when the practices of today may not be what is taught in pre-service classrooms. Not only is it necessary to stay up on relevant trends, but also relevant emotional needs of the profession. The student I watched, who struggled with the idea of leaving the profession, was also struggling with the needs of diverse students. This student felt she had no one who saw her during her supervision and wondered how she could connect with her students. This topic would have been ideal to work through with her supervisor, but there was no room for that type of reflection or intentional conversation in her classes.

The field of instructional supervision is intended to prepare educators who can withstand the nature of the education profession. Many have turned to supervision models that incorporate structured feedback. However, supervision is more than promoting reflective practice in pre- and post-conferences.

The field of instructional supervision should attempt to stay ahead of the educational field and no longer trail behind the trends. It is essential for the vitality of the profession. Young teachers today are faced with being culturally sensitive, tending to the decay of the emotional resilience of society, while staying relevant compared to YouTube videos and AI teaching. This can put a great deal of pressure on people who are not used to a traditional workforce. Therefore, the field of instructional supervision should consider the "whole teacher," just as an accomplished teacher would consider the whole student. This includes pre-service teachers' emotional and motivational practices for longevity. It also includes culturally relevant practices allowing students to embrace themselves and respect others. In the field of education, we expect teachers to know that every student is unique and learns at a different pace. We should expect supervisors to see every teacher as unique as well.

Carl Glickman (1980) proposed that there are different stages of instructional supervision. This concept has become more and more relevant as adults in the workforce demand that their individual needs be recognized and at least considered. Supervisors can aid pre-service teachers by individualizing observations to capture their uniqueness as adults and use those observations to develop appropriate supervision for the individual.

I have noticed that many teachers require much practice and coaching to learn all that is required to be considered "excellent." As a campus administrator, I cannot afford to leave coaching to the mentor teacher or the instructional specialist. I have often created a team to assist teachers in need of assistance based on their learning styles. Instructional supervision cannot be considered a "one size" fits all profession, as all pre-service teachers will require different support to be successful. This will allow pre-service teachers to understand a multi-faceted approach for their students. Due to the many facets of education, a multi-disciplinary approach during supervision is key, including experts from other departments imparting knowledge about mental health, trauma informed care, and trends of culture and learning. This approach would be more than a class, but an opportunity to work with others in the separate fields to understand how this may come together in their classrooms.

Pre-service teachers need to feel as though they can collaborate with and confide in their instructional supervisor. There is still a delicate balance between coaching and evaluation (Gallavan, 2020). Gallavan discussed that there needs to be a level of humility and vulnerability in the relationship between instructional supervisors and teachers. This trusted approach allowed me to aid the aforementioned teacher when her instructional supervisor failed her. It was important to allow the teacher to see herself as a person and not just an educational machine. I believe that the field of instructional supervision should develop this aspect of pre-service teachers as they embark on their journey to become an educator. This will require the field to not only develop practices of strong pedagogy but also develop other aspects of human development of adults, in areas of self-awareness, coping with stress, and opportunity to face hidden trauma within oneself.

In conclusion, the field of supervision is responsible for preparing the educators of tomorrow, if educators are to prepare children for the future. This also means that the field should account for pre-service teachers' internal and external obstacles and find ways to assist in overcoming them.

References

Gallavan, N. P. (2020). When extraordinary circumstances yield exceptional consequences: The importance of readiness, receptiveness, and responsiveness. *International Journal of Multidisciplinary Perspectives in Higher Education.* vol. 5.no. 1. p. 184. *Gale Academic OneFile*, link.gale.com/apps/doc/A641420983/AONE?u=txshrpub100386&sid=bookmark-AONE&xid=b68772c0. Accessed 6 Oct. 2023.

Gale Document Number: GALE|A641420983

Glickman, Carl D. (1980). The developmental approach to supervision: Supervisors should recognize stages of professional development and treat teachers as individuals. *Educational Leadership: Association for Supervision and Curriculum Development.* *https://files.ascd.org/staticfiles/ascd/pdf/journals/ed_lead/el_198011_glickman.pdf*

Supervisors, Supervision, and LGBTQ+ Educators

Jim Nolan

Dr. Jim Nolan, a former elementary teacher, secondary teacher, and guidance counselor retired in June 2015 from Penn State University after serving as the Hermanowicz Professor of Teacher Education and the Co-Coordinator of the Elementary Professional Development School Partnership between Penn State University and the State College Area School District. His work in the field of supervision focused on practice-based strategies such as clinical supervision and peer coaching that aim at enhancing teacher reflection, decision-making, and autonomy. He is co-author with Dr. Linda Hoover of *Teacher Supervision and Evaluation: Theory into Practice.* During his graduate studies at Penn State, Jim studied supervision with Dr. Lee Goldsberry who introduced him to COPIS.

This think piece was inspired by an email I received from a teacher with whom I had worked for several years and admired as a teacher and a person.[12] The email motivated me to think about this topic, to do a little bit of reading, and to end up with far

---

[12] In this think piece I feel obliged to protect the teacher's identity as much as possible, so I use "they" pronouns, even to the point of rephrasing the pronouns in the original email. I recognize that using "they" as opposed to "he/she" hides some of the nuances that result in different attitudes towards and different characterizations of male and female LGBTQ+ educators. Nevertheless, protecting the teacher must come first.

more questions than answers. So, what I am attempting to do here is to provoke a conversation by providing some context including the message, summarizing some of the things I learned from reading, and posing a number of questions that I can't yet answer but seem worthy of voicing.

Some Context

I had supervised student interns in this teacher's elementary classroom and saw first-hand the teacher's caring for students and ability to create a classroom environment in which each child felt welcome and benefitted from excellent instruction. In addition, I had witnessed this teacher presenting important information about classroom learning environments to our interns for several years. I saw this teacher as an excellent teacher.

During the time I worked with this teacher, I knew they were gay. I was also aware that the teacher's close colleagues knew they were gay. The teacher did not "come out" to the school community or to the community at large as far as I knew. In August of 2023, this teacher received an invitation to come to a first-day-of-school luncheon with other retired teachers from the building where they had worked. The teacher's response to the invitation shocked me:

> I debated sharing this with you, but I will do so. I am very upset with a number of my former colleagues in the group and what they continue to support. What they have supported has left me feeling too humiliated to come and break bread with them.
>
> The culture wars in the last year have been very upsetting to me as a gay person. I've had to sit by as Fox News and conservative political figures have continually maligned teachers like me, calling us "groomers" and saying that we sexualize children. Knowing that several people in the group have actively campaigned for candidates like Mastriano and Trump is deeply wounding to me. I question a person's friendship when they actively campaign to put into

power legislators who plan to take away my right to marry and to adopt a child. If they have issues with those rights, they certainly at some level don't feel I should have been teaching children.

I was hoping after the pandemic to do some more tutoring and subbing but knowing that the schools where I offered these services—in XXX County—are in such a red area where everyone listens to Fox News, I am just too frightened to continue to work with children. Last summer I donated all my teaching and tutoring materials to a local charter school. I wouldn't want to risk being accused of something when so many people in the area know I am gay and have been brainwashed.

This email made me feel sad and guilty. Though I had often considered the turmoil that would be created internally by having to continually hide an important aspect of one's identity, I had never really considered in any great detail the emotional impact of living and working in a community where at least a portion of the community, including one's school colleagues, saw one's identity as potentially harmful and threatening to children. The current backlash against the LGBTQ+ community has clearly forced this teacher to rethink the meaning of their entire career and legacy. It struck me as especially sad because they did not have children of their own, so the children in their classroom provided the primary possibility for leaving a legacy. In addition, the current backlash has resulted in their choice to not tutor children who would definitely have benefitted from their knowledge and expertise. The sadness that this email provoked forced me to think about what my response would have been if I were this teacher's supervisor and what supervisors and supervision as a field should be doing in response to the current backlash against the LGBTQ+ community.

I had always taken comfort in the bumper sticker that reads, "Think globally, act locally." With regard to matters of diversity, equity, inclusion and social justice, I interpreted it to mean that as an individual I needed to be as supportive and encouraging as possible in my teaching and supervising with all individuals, but especially with those from marginalized groups. I saw that as acting locally, and it was something I worked at. I was being a local and personal ally. Global action seemed just too big for me, too complicated, too far removed from individual classrooms, teachers, and students. I was willing to leave the macro issues to somebody else. There were others who would be allies on the global scale. Since my retirement and the opportunity that it presents to think about the bigger picture without the demands of everyday work on the local level, I have recognized that my response to caring for marginalized people was absolutely inadequate. So, as a supervisor and someone who hoped to be a leader in the field of instructional supervision, what should have been my response to the antagonism and bigotry against the LGBTQ+ community? My most honest answer to that question is I don't know exactly, but it should have been different and more.

Because I believe that scholarly literature can be enlightening and helpful, I decided to turn to the literature on instructional supervision and the LGBTQ+ community to see what the literature had to say. I did not find any scholarly articles that were identified through my searches of supervision, instructional supervision, and LGBTQ+ teachers/educators. Admittedly, I am a bit rusty on searches so that could be my fault. I did see articles that focused on supervision of counseling of LGBTQ+ programs and supervision of group work using an LGBTQ+ model as well as an article on the supervisory experiences of psychology interns who identified as LGBTQ+. I also found articles that focused on school leadership and LGBTQ+ students and culturally responsive teaching, but none that focused primarily on leadership and supervision in reference to LGBTQ+ educators. Though I admit that I may have missed some writing that directly links these topics, I am left thinking there really is not a significant body of literature in that area. I am wondering if and why that is the case. Surely supervisors of both in-service and pre-service teachers have supervised teachers who identified as members of the LGBTQ+ community. There must also be supervisors who identify as LGBTQ+. Given the stressful situation that these educators can find themselves in, especially in communities that are openly hostile, there must be questions and dilemmas that supervisors struggle to deal with. Is the percentage of the educator population so small, that the problems are not significant? Do supervisors feel that their role is working with the individual teachers and leaving the macro issues to others as I did? Is it too risky to write about these issues?

Legal Status of LGBTQ+ Educators

I did find literature that focused on the legal status of LGBTQ+ educators. From these articles I learned that 28 states currently do not have laws that protect the working rights of LGBTQ+ people (Associated Press, 2019), and that a record 70 bills were introduced in state legislatures in 2023 that were antagonistic to the LGBTQ+ community (Peele, 2023). In states where legal protection is not afforded by state law, the status of LGBTQ+ educators is typically decided by the courts. Historically, there seem to be two key concepts that courts consider when schools attempt to dismiss a teacher because of the teacher's sexual orientation— "exemplar and nexus." (DeMitchell, Eckes and Fossey, 2009).

Exemplar refers to the long-standing belief that teachers serve as role models for their students and, therefore, have an obligation to conduct themselves, both in and out of school, in ways that are representative of good moral character. Because they serve as exemplars, teachers' personal lives can be used in determining their fitness for teaching as a career. Many court cases focused on the dismissal of LGTBQ+ teachers used the concept of exemplar alone to revoke teaching licenses. One of the most famous of these cases, *Gaylord v. Tacoma* that was decided in 1975, involved a teacher who had been rated as an effective teacher with no issues for 12 years. However, once it became public that he was gay, the teacher was dismissed. The court held that because this teacher was comfortable with being gay and had chosen not to pursue psychiatric help to change his sexual orientation, he was therefore morally responsible for this personal choice and upheld the dismissal (DeMitchell, Eckes and Fossey, 2009).

The concept of nexus implies that exemplar alone is insufficient to dismiss an LGBTQ+ teacher in some situations. To dismiss a teacher on such grounds, the school must show a clear connection between the teacher's personal life and impaired teaching performance. In

Morrison v. State Board of Education, a case that was decided in 1969, the California State Supreme Court overturned lower court rulings that supported the dismissal of a gay teacher on the grounds that a clear connection to ineffective performance had not been established. In its opinion, the Court found that the notion of dismissing a teacher simply on the grounds that their personal life is immoral violates the teacher's rights. The court supported its opinion in these words, "Today's morals may be tomorrow's ancient and absurd customs, and conversely conduct socially acceptable today may be anathema tomorrow" (DeMitchell, Eckes and Fossey, 2009).

The U.S. Supreme Court did take a major step forward in potentially protecting LGBTQ+ educators from being dismissed simply because of their sexual identity in *Bostock v. Clayton County*, a case in which a Clayton County employee in Georgia had been fired from his job for joining a gay softball league. In a 6-3 ruling where the majority included justices Gorsuch, Roberts, Ginsburg, Breyer, Kagan and Sotomayor, the court ruled that Title VII of the Civil Rights Act of 1964 provides equal treatment under the law for LGBTQ+ workers and ordered Bostock reinstated (Supreme Court Syllabus, 2020). Citing this court decision, the Biden Administration issued an executive order in 2021 that stated that LGBTQ+ educators and students were entitled to equal treatment under Title IX of the Education Amendments of 1972 but also suggested that determining the nature of equal treatment was in the hands of local school boards and educators (Federal Register, 2021).

While the U.S. Supreme Court decision and the Biden Executive Memorandum provide some assurance of job protection for LGBTQ+ educators, events in recent years make clear that administrative executive orders can be easily reversed, and even long-standing court precedents can be overturned. It is also noteworthy that the *Bostock* case involved a county employee, not a teacher. County employees are not held to the same exemplar standard as teachers in the eyes of the courts. Without clear protection by state or federal law, it is difficult to say whether any individual court will weigh exemplar or nexus more heavily in deciding whether a dismissal is justified. Additionally, in communities that have a strong anti-LGBTQ+ sentiment even courts that lean on the connection between personal life and impaired teaching may be persuaded that the general sentiment in the community is so strong that it will result in a lack of public and student confidence and even animosity towards the teacher leading to ineffective performance. It is also important to note that non-tenured teachers who identify as LGBTQ+ are in significantly greater peril due to the power differential and burden of proof in a dismissal process. What is the role of instructional supervisors or school leaders in working with LGBTQ+ educators who find themselves in this precarious legal position? Should supervisors as a group and supervision as a field advocate for state laws that protect gay educators?

Outness, Teaching, and Role Models

I also found an interesting article that studied the experiences of teachers from the LGB community (Simons, Hahn, Pepe & Russell, 2021). From an earlier survey study of 191 teachers who identified as LGB, these researchers selected 24 educators from different age cohorts for phenomenological interviews. The 24 educators came from school districts near Austin, Tucson, New York City, and San Francisco. The authors using a framework from Jackson (2007) developed a description of three levels of "outness." Level One educators had made no disclosures about their personal lives. They attempted to keep their personal and teaching lives completely separate, often because they perceived that they were in a precarious position. Some of the educators at this level decided to leave the profession. Level Two educators engaged in selective disclosure. They disclosed their sexual orientation with close colleagues, typically only when they were asked directly about it. Many educators in Levels One and Two were careful about the pedagogical approaches that they used. They preferred to be similar rather than different from other colleagues in terms of their teaching approaches. They worried about standing out. Many felt they could not be what they wanted to be. (Interestingly, although the teacher who sent me the email message would have been classified as Level 2 in terms of outness, they felt free to use approaches that made them stand out in a very positive way.)

Level Three educators engaged in full disclosure. These teachers openly disclosed their sexual orientation with colleagues and also disclosed to high school students when asked directly about it. Their major motivation in disclosure was a desire to be visible rather than invisible, to be role models for all students, including those who identify as LGBTQ+, and to enhance social justice. They saw themselves as helping others by serving as role models. They also felt comfortable in experimenting with a wide variety of teaching approaches and were confident that they were free to match their teaching to what students needed. One of the critical factors in helping these educators to engage in full disclosure was the presence of other adults who supported them. Often the support came from both family and other educators in the school environment.

This article struck a deep chord with me. I was surprised, though I probably should not have been, by the fact that many of these teachers who came almost exclusively from large metropolitan environments still felt a sense of precariousness about their position as teachers. How much more precarious must be the lives of LGBTQ+ educators in smaller rural communities that are traditionally much more conservative and more openly hostile? In addition to being threatened on a personal level in terms of keeping their jobs, these teachers also felt handcuffed in terms of experimentation with pedagogical approaches. Their precariousness led them to attempt to blend in, rather than stand out. That seems to me to be a very natural outcome of the precariousness of the environment. In contrast, teachers who were fully disclosing felt comfortable using a variety of pedagogical approaches and were confident that they were better able to meet student needs as a result. While their students most likely benefited from this freedom, the students of teachers at Levels One and Two may well have been shortchanged by their teachers' perceived need to blend in with colleagues. This is clearly related to the fundamental task of instructional supervision, enhancing the learning and development of students, but what does supervisor behavior in that situation look like? What can supervisors do to support those teachers who are not willing to disclose their sexual orientation or to mitigate the impact that it might be having on their teaching? What can supervisors do at the district level or state level to reduce the threat and allow teachers to teach in ways that seem both authentic to them and helpful to students?

The notion of LGBTQ+ educators acting as role models for students who identify as LGBTQ+ also made me think more deeply about the issue. We all understand the value of having role models, especially individuals who seem like us who have demonstrated the possibility for success. While not necessary, having a teacher who is a role model appears to have important benefits for students. Teach for America does have a page on its website that provides testimony from current educators about the impact of having a teacher who identified as LGBTQ+ when they were students (Zing, 2020). One teacher, Kristol, wrote, "I remember thinking wow, look at her. She's an adult and she's out and people don't care. She is confident in her sexual orientation and who she is. And she was unapologetically herself." Kristol added, "I remember thinking, I want to be like that." Another educator, Adam, wrote, "One of the first teachers I had who identified as LGBTQ was in high school. They incorporated a lot of literature that was both dynamic and explored sexual identity and brought out the humanity of the characters that they chose to analyze within that class. I think for me it was really, really helpful to feel like I was appreciated. Like I was seen, heard, and visible." Of the five educators who posted about their experiences on the website, Kristol and Adam are the only ones who had role models in high school. The other three responses discuss how the presence of such a role model would have been helpful.

We have long used the concept of the power of role models as one argument for developing a more racially and ethnically diverse teaching force in the United States. Do LGBTQ+ students not need role models, too? What can supervisors and school leaders do to create environments in which LGBTQ+ students have experiences working with teachers who are role models in that aspect of their identity? I also wondered why it is so much more acceptable to talk about the needs of LGBTQ+ students than it is to talk about the needs of LGBTQ+ educators. Why is it ok to think about helping these students and simultaneously pretend that these educators and the challenges they face do not exist?

Advocacy and Support for LGBTQ+ Educators

The web page from Teach for America cited above was one of the few examples that I was able to find in terms of national advocacy and support for LGBTQ+ educators from within the mainstream educational community. The National Education Association does have web pages that provide advice on legal issues for LGBTQ+ educators but no network or support group that I was able to find. When I searched the website of the American Federation of Teachers, I was able to find no resources for teachers from the LGBTQ+ community. This may well be due to my faulty search techniques, but resources do not appear to be plentiful within mainstream teacher organizations. The Gay Lesbian and Straight Educational Network (GLSEN) founded in the 1990s does provide support for LGBTQ+ students, educators, and families and strives to create affirming school environments and to end discrimination, harassment and bullying based on sexual orientation, gender identity, and gender expression through its national network and through its 43 chapters in 30 states (GLSEN, 2023). This organization does provide a wide variety of resources; however, the focus appears to be much more oriented towards serving students and their families than educators.

In rather stark contrast, the National Association of Secondary School Principals has a network for LGBTQ school leaders. The purpose of the network is stated in this way,

> The challenging work of school leadership can often feel isolating—especially if you identify as LGBTQ+. To provide a platform of mutual support for principals and assistant principals in the LGBTQ+ community, NASSP manages a network where administrators can meet regularly to share challenges, struggles, and opportunities, and support each other both personally and professionally. (National Association of Secondary School Principals, 2023)

The site includes testimony and stories from school leaders as well as resources and provides the opportunity for school leaders to join the network. In addition, NASSP has a position statement affirming the rights of LGBTQ+ students, teachers, and administrators. I did not find any specific resources or information concerning how administrators could support LGBTQ+ educators through supervision or other leadership tasks. In fact, the majority of recommendations, guiding principles, and resources are focused on providing, safe and welcoming environments and inclusive curricula for LGBTQ+ students. NASSP should be applauded for its support for the LGBTQ+ community, but again we see a much stronger emphasis on supporting LGBTQ+ students as opposed to teachers. I also find it puzzling that similar kinds of public advocacy and support are not so apparent among the leading national teacher organizations.

Closing without Closure

Clearly supervisors and the field of instructional supervision have an obligation to support and encourage all educators, especially those from all marginalized groups. In my view that is a domain that has not been fully explored in the literature nor addressed in practice except at an individual level. The email from my teacher friend has provided me with the opportunity to think more deeply about the plight of LGBTQ+ educators, maybe for the very first time. LGBTQ+ teachers are clearly not the only marginalized group of educators within the United States; however, their challenges seem somewhat unique to me in at least three ways. First, it is not only possible but even praiseworthy in some communities to espouse strident moral opposition to LGBTQ+ educators simply because of who they are. Second, their legal situation within the courts seems somewhat more precarious than members of other marginalized groups. I am not suggesting that people from other marginalized groups are treated fairly within the court system, but rather that the law itself, as opposed to its unfair application, puts LGBTQ+ educators at risk. Third, in contrast to other marginalized groups, it is quite possible for some percentage of LGBTQ+ educators to hide their identities, i.e., "to pass," and pretend that they are not who they really are even though the personal and pedagogical cost of hiding their identities may be quite high. Though I am not sure what the answers are or what the most helpful actions by supervisors or scholars in the field of supervision might be, I am convinced that these are questions we should grapple with as an intellectual community.

References

_____ (2021) Executive order preventing and combatting discrimination on the basis of gender identity or sexual orientation. *Federal Register* January 2021.

_____ (2023) GLSEN https://www.glsen.org/

Associated Press (2019) *AP analysis: Most states lack laws protecting LGBT workers. https://apnews.com/article/8b5086b09b9042bf808d82108b7d925c*

DeMitchell, T., Eckes, S., & Fossey, R. (2009) Sexual orientation and the public school teacher. *Public Interest Law Journal 19*, pp. 65-104.

Jackson, J. M. (2007) *Unmasking identities: An exploration of the lives of gay and lesbian teachers.* Lanham, MD: Lexington Books.

National Association of Secondary School Principals (2023) *NASSP LGBTQ+ School Leaders Network.* https://www.nassp.org/leadership-networks/lgbtq-school-leaders-network

Peele, C. (2023) Roundup *of anti-LGBTQ+ legislation advancing in states across the country.* https://www.hrc.org/press-releases/roundup-of-anti-lgbtq-legislation-advancing-in-states-across-the-country

Simons, J., Hahn, S., Pope, M., & Russell, S. (2021) Experiences of educators who identify as lesbian, gay and bisexual. *Journal of Gay and Lesbian Social Services 33*(3), 300-319.

Syllabus Supreme Court of the United States (2020) *No 17-1618 Bostock v. Clayton County, Georgia certiorari to the United States Court of Appeals for the Eleventh Circuit.* https://www.supremecourt.gov/opinions/19pdf/17-1618_hfci.pdf

Zingg, L. (2020) I see me: Representation of LGBTQ+ teachers in the classroom. *Teach for America.* https://www.teachforamerica.org/one-day/top-issues/i-see-me-representation-of-lgbtq-teachers-in-the-classroom.

The Unintentional Consequences of "Supervision" and "Supervisor"

Yanira Oliveras

Dr. Yanira Oliveras is an associate professor in the School of Education at The University of Texas at Tyler. Prior to joining the UT Tyler faculty in 2014, she spent 20 years in K-12 education where she served as a teacher, curriculum coordinator, and school principal. Dr. Oliveras' research agenda and service focuses on the advancement of instructional leadership and supervision in Belize. She is the recipient of a CARSI grant from the US Embassy Belmopan to collaborate with the Belize Ministry of Education in building teachers and school leaders' instructional supervision capacity. She also works with the Belize Ministry of Education's Teacher Education Unit to redesign teacher preparation program and newly qualified teacher induction. As part of her work in Belize, she developed and validated the *Instructional Supervision Sense of Efficacy* scale. Dr. Oliveras holds a B.S. in Elementary Education, M.Ed. and Ph.D. in Curriculum and Instruction from Penn State University. She was admitted into COPIS in 2017 and studied under Drs. Jim Nolan and Bernard Badiali. As a member of COPIS, she served as secretary in 2021-2022 and Chair in 2022-2023.

As the implementation and value of instructional coaching are on the rise in Belize, the unintentional negative impact the terms "supervision" and "supervisor" have on the supervision process has been at the forefront of the discourse among educators and senior education administrators. While the depth of dialogue around this issue in Belize is new, this debate is not new to the field of supervision nor is supervision new to Belize. In *Supervision in Transition*, over three decades ago, Glickman (1992) stressed that the term supervision had negative connotations resulting in dislike of the process as it is perceived as an inspectional process with a focus on weaknesses. The negative connotations and history of supervision in Belize significantly influence the perceptions and implementation of the supervision process as a new supervision model and capacity-building efforts are on their way across the country.

The new model for instructional supervision in Belize was designed in alignment with Cogan's clinical supervision model to help teachers improve teaching (Cogan, 1973) by engaging in the formal supervision cycle with the goal of facilitating improvement through collaboration between the teacher and supervisor (Goldhammer, 1969). The Belize supervision model was also developed emphasizing that, irrespective of its structure, supervision's primary focus should be on directing teachers to engage in reflection on their instructional practices and enhancing their comprehension of learning processes, their role as educators, and avenues for professional growth (Sergiovanni et al., 2013). Furthermore, the model was designed in alignment with Gall and Acheson's (2010) three key objectives for clinical supervision, as articulated by Zepeda (2018, pg. 25): (1) furnishing teachers with objective feedback, (2) addressing instructional challenges, and (3) assisting teachers in honing their teaching skills.

Over time, the nature of supervision in the United States has evolved from clinical or instructional oversight to instructional leadership across diverse settings. In the U.S., educators have increasingly embraced a more democratic approach, placing value on teachers' expertise and fostering conversations guided by teachers' self-reflection on their practices (Glanz, 2018; Mette et al., 2017). Conversely, in Belize, a perception persists among educators that supervision is primarily a hierarchical oversight procedure rather than a collaborative and reflective one. While Belizeans embrace and believe the shift is needed, their cognitive dissonance aligns with Glickman's argument in 1992, in which he acknowledged that the impact of the term "supervisor" on the supervision process cannot be disregarded.

The instructional supervision model and tools chosen for the redesigned implementation of instructional supervision in Belize were specifically crafted to furnish supervisors and school leaders with a framework for carrying out "an organizational function concerned with teacher growth, leading to improvement in teaching performance and greater student learning" (Nolan & Hoover, 2011, p. 6). The instructional supervision cycle encompasses a pre-observation conference, a comprehensive classroom observation, and a post-observation conference (Cogan, 1973; Goldhammer, 1969; Zepeda, 2018). During the classroom observation, the supervisor is tasked with gathering data, which is then utilized to inform the subsequent post-observation conference (Goldhammer, 1969; Zepeda, 2018), aiming to support the teacher in enhancing both teaching methods and student learning.

However, given the historical context and hierarchical nature of supervision in Belize, when presented with the new processes, expectations, and tools, field supervisors and teacher educators argued that evaluation of the lessons and explicitly telling teachers what they had to improve were crucial parts of the supervision process. Belizean teachers expect immediate feedback upon the conclusion of the lesson focused on what they had done well and what they could improve. The contextual implications led to extended conversations with educators and senior administrators on how to move away from directive conferences to collaborative post-observation conferences where the teachers are guided to reflect on their teaching. How does the country move away from summative to formative feedback that leads to self-reflection rather than directives issued by the supervisor?

It is crucial to highlight that efforts to transition to collaborative post-conferences took place simultaneously with the release of a new national curriculum focused on student-centered instruction and competency-based learning The curriculum transition was another drastic shift for the Belize education system since the main instructional method used by teachers at all levels had been teacher-centered, whole group instruction often referred to as "chalk and talk." Hence, in addition to the conversations and capacity-building efforts focused on instructional supervision, the team also engaged educators in conversations about research-based, student-centered instructional practices. The shift in the instructional expectations for teachers further complicated the context as not only were supervisors new to the idea of guiding self-reflection and allowing teachers to identify effective practices and areas for improvement, but they were also developing their own understanding of competency-based education. The instructional supervisors' learning curve was steep while teachers looked to them for explicit guidance on how to transition from teacher-centric instruction to student-centered classrooms.

The Dissonance Became Discernable

From the beginning of the project, during the evaluation of the current state of teacher education and planning for an intervention, the team understood the importance of in-depth training and follow-up. Supervisors, teacher educators, and school leaders need a strong conceptual understanding of the new supervision model and expectations for the processes to be implemented with fidelity and to increase the chances of a successful transition. During the initial three-day session with university-based supervisors and teacher educators, I presented the agenda to the attendees and provided a brief overview of our definition of supervision,

- Instructional supervision is the process of supporting teacher growth through a cycle of observation, feedback, coaching, and reflective inquiry.
- The purpose is to improve student outcomes through developing better instructional practices that are used consistently in every classroom.
- Evaluation is the process of assessing a teacher's practices and effectiveness.
- Supervision is the process of facilitating a teacher's professional growth based on data collected through classroom observations. (Oliveras et al, 2021).

During the time I had allotted for questions after the introductory overview, a veteran teacher-educator raised his hand and stated, "I have been an educator for over 40 years. How is the instructional supervision model and process you are proposing any different from what we have been doing for pre-service teachers for decades?"

I had been warned that this educator would push back on any changes or suggestions that there was a need for significant improvement in the support pre-service teachers were provided. As an outsider and a Puerto Rican in my 30th year of education in the United States, my eight years of experiences and work in Belize were limited in comparison to the extensive experience and depth of knowledge of the educators I stood in front of. I was aware of the possibility that in their eyes, my awareness and understanding of their system and history were insignificant. However, my understanding and observations were not superficial, so I took a risk and said, "With all due respect, you have decades of experience as an evaluator, not an instructional supervisor." While later some expressed their annoyance at the Belizean educator's challenging question and perceived it as an attempt to purposefully undermine my authority in the field, he provided the attendees and me with the opportunity to explore the reality of the context in which we work, which resulted in an in-depth discussion based on the attendees' reflections of their own practices and experiences with supervision.

Although his question set the stage for the need for change, he raised an important issue that needed to be deconstructed and addressed. How is this "new" supervision different from what supervisors and teachers know and expect? As we delved into the process and skills needed for supervision to be effectively enacted, an experienced field supervisor said, "I'm the supervisor. I'm there to provide the newly qualified teacher with the guidance they need. They look to me for expertise and directives for change." Another experienced educator who had recently earned an advanced education degree added:

> The instructional supervisor is the expert. At the end
> of the observation, I expect her to tell me what I did
> well and how I can improve. I want to know how I can
> improve and learn from her expertise and experience.

Throughout the project (August 2021–December 2022), supervisors and teachers alike continued to grapple with the idea that teachers, regardless of their years of experience, can and should engage in self-reflection without relying solely on supervisors to provide guidance. Moreover, the documentation collected during the observations should be used as evidence to help teachers engage in self-reflection and not as evidence of wrongdoing. We were simultaneously asking teachers to transition to student-centered instruction, to release the responsibility of learning and allow students to own their learning; while asking supervisors to release responsibility of learning and allow teachers to own their learning and growth. However, supervisors were not the only ones skeptical about this process.

As part of the training and learning process, we watched pre- and post-observation conference videos. My co-trainers and I modeled conferencing during role play and with Belizean teachers in their schools. While modeling how to lead a post-observation conference at a local school, I asked the teacher questions about the lesson focused on her professional learning goals as well as about the observed practices that she could reinforce and improve upon. While the teacher answered my questions and engaged in some self-reflection, she continuously went back to two troubling questions, "How did I do?" and "What do you want me to change?" Telling the teacher that I would prefer not to answer those questions as I wanted her to tell me how the lesson went and how she could improve in the future was frustrating for the teacher. Asking teachers to reflect and share their thoughts on the lessons was completely foreign and uncomfortable for teachers and supervisors alike. Their experiences related to supervision emphasized what Glickman said over three decades ago, the influence of the term "supervisor" on the supervision process cannot be ignored.

In the aforementioned instances, the educators perceived the instructional supervisor as the evaluator, the individual in charge of assessing the teachers' performance, and the administrator who monitored the teaching of the curriculum and enforced the use of the preferred instructional practices. At the beginning, not one of the educators (teachers and supervisors) expected teachers to reflect, actively participate, and enhance their instructional practices after engaging in the supervision process. The dissonance between their experiences with supervision and the instructional supervision cycle I spoke of prevented them from grasping the idea of instructional supervision as U.S. supervision schools know it. However, after reflecting on the context and the continuous struggle with making the shift in their thinking, I presented the ideas as instructional coaching. The supervisors and teachers had a clearer understanding of the coaching processes and practices and how those could lead to the teachers' professional growth versus the "new" instructional supervision concepts. I was astonished by the ease with which they embraced the idea of coaching but struggled to accept the idea that supervisors coach teachers.

While briefing the senior leaders of the Belize Ministry of Education about the project, known as Instructional Supervision for Educational Excellence in Belize (i-SEE Belize), and the progress the team was making towards the national implementation of instructional supervision, we discussed the challenges the team was facing due to the misunderstanding surrounding instructional supervision, and the false sense of positive efficacy among of field supervisors. Supervisors assumed they were expected to evaluate teachers and lead directive post-observation conferences; their efficacy and indeed their capacity to be directive was high. However, when asked to be facilitators of self-reflection through questioning, their efficacy declined. They became self-conscious when modeling post-observation conferences as they struggled to facilitate reflection. After outlining plans for follow-up sessions and coaching for the supervisors and school leaders, the highest-ranking member of the leadership team, said, "We need to stop using instructional 'supervision' to facilitate the shift from evaluation to supervision. We must use instructional coaching, a concept that is broadly understood as a supportive process." The next session was titled, "Instructional Coaching" a session for supervisors and teacher educators.

To Ponder: Are we to forego the terms "Supervision" and "Supervisor"?

- How many educators, school leaders, and scholars misunderstand the processes?

- How is the use of "supervisor" and "supervision" impacting the depth and growth of our field when instructional coaching is commonly understood?

- How many practitioners and scholars think of instructional coaching as instructional supervision while so many think of supervision as managerial and evaluative?

- How is "supervision" affecting our membership and the number of proposals submitted for our SIG's sessions in AERA?

- Are we missing valuable opportunities to engage in the work, in research and collaboration by using "supervision" rather than "coaching"?

As an instructional supervision advocate and scholar, I grapple with these questions and whether to reluctantly relinquish the terms supervision and supervisor.

References

Cogan, M. (1973). *Clinical supervision.* Boston, MA: Houghton Mifflin.

Glanz, J. (2018). Chronicling Perspectives about the State of Instructional Supervision by Eight Prominent Scholars of Supervision. *Journal of Educational Supervision, 1*(1). Retrieved from https://digitalcommons.library.umaine.edu/jes/vol1/iss1/1

Glickman, C.D. (Ed.). (1992*). Supervision in transition: The 1992 ASCD yearbook.* Alexandria, VA: Association for Supervision and Curriculum Development.

Goldhammer, R. (1969). *Clinical supervision: Special methods for the supervision of teachers.* New York: Holt, Rinehart, and Winston.

Mette, I. M., Range, B. G., Anderson, J., Hvidston, D. J., Nieuwenhuizen, L, & Doty, J. (2017). The wicked problem of the intersection between supervision and evaluation. *International Electronic Journal of Elementary Education, 9*(3), 709-724. doi: 10.1155/2012/490647

Nolan, J., Jr., & Hoover, L. A. (2011). *Teacher supervision and evaluation: Theory into practice* (3rd ed.). Hoboken, NJ: John Wiley & Sons.

Oliveras-Ortiz, Y., Hickey, W. D., Kaiser, F. J., & Lane, J. (2021). Instructional Supervisors Guide: Instructional supervision for educational excellence in Belize. Belize City: Belize Ministry of Education, Culture, Science, and Technology.

Sergiovanni, T. J., Starratt, R. J., & Cho, V. (2013). *Supervision: A redefinition* (9th ed.). New York, NY: McGraw-Hill.

Zepeda, S.J, & Ponticell, J.A. (Eds.). (2018). *The Wiley handbook of educational supervision.* New York: Wiley-Blackwell.

Where Have All the Teachers Gone?

A REFLECTION ON SUPERVISION IN RURAL SPACES

Noelle A. Paufler

Noelle A. Paufler, PhD is Associate Professor–P-12 Educational Leadership and the Program Coordinator for the Doctor of Education in Education Systems Improvement Science at Clemson University. Her research interests include K-12 educational policy, specifically how educational leaders enact policy into practice, its impact on teachers and students, and implications for leadership preparation. Her current research examines the lived experiences of evaluators and teachers related to the development, implementation, and impact/(un)intended consequences of teacher evaluation systems in P-12 and higher education settings. Additional areas of her research focus on doctoral leadership preparation, specifically preparing leaders who have the knowledge, skills, and systems perspective needed to effectively serve in rural school communities. She has experience as a high school social studies teacher, district administrator, and applied researcher in high-need districts and schools. She earned her doctorate at Arizona State University under the supervision of Dr. Audrey Amrein-Beardsley and has been a member of the Council of Professors of Instruction Supervision since 2020.

T his piece reflects my current thinking on the evolution of the field of instructional supervision in the narrow context of my research on leadership development in rural South Carolina. In retrospect, the invitation to write a think piece has encouraged me to consider how three current research projects intersect around supervision, leadership coaching, and doctoral leadership preparation in rural spaces. This is a work in progress. For background context, I will start with an overview of the research projects.

> **Teachers' Perceptions of the Qualities of Effective Supervisors.** As part of a survey research study, Stephen P. Gordon (TX), Mary Lynne Derrington (TN), and I are examining teachers' perceptions of effective supervisor qualities during the post-observation conference. In a survey recently administered to teachers across our three respective states, we asked teachers to rate the importance of various supervisor qualities (e.g., relational trust, authenticity). I am hopeful that what we learn from this study will help strengthen leadership preparation, particularly for principals serving in rural school communities.

> **Leading Educational Administrator Development for Excellent Rural Schools Center of Excellence.** As part of a three-year research project funded by the South Carolina Commission on Higher Education, Clemson University colleagues, Hans W. Klar (Director) and Angela D. Carter (Co-Director), and I are working with a team to develop a model for preparing leadership coaches who can support school leaders in the use of improvement science. The goal is to help leaders in rural, underperforming, and high-poverty schools improve education systems in ways that increase teacher retention and student learning outcomes.

> **Preparing Leaders to Address Systemic, Complex Challenges in High-Needs Settings.** As the program

coordinator for the Doctor of Education (EdD) in Education Systems Improvement Science at Clemson University, I am collaborating with faculty colleagues on continuous program improvement. The EdD Program seeks to improve access to educational leadership preparation by providing a pathway to an education doctorate for diverse, historically underrepresented graduate students, particularly those serving in rural regions of the state. Through our research, we are looking for ways to better prepare leaders with the skills they need to lead systems-level change, improve their experiences in preparation, and support application of their learning.

As I began to draft this think piece, I reflected on supervision in terms of who it serves and how it functions. At the most superficial level, I could not help but start with the most pressing current challenge facing many of the EdD students at Clemson University and the participants in the LEADERS Center—teacher retention. We know that there is a teacher shortage everywhere, especially in rural schools. South Carolina is no exception. So, what does supervision have to do with it? How can we develop school leaders who are prepared to supervise teachers in ways that first and foremost encourage good teachers to remain in the classroom and second help them develop as professional educators?

Background

Each year, nearly 300,000 teachers across the nation leave the profession—two-thirds before they have reached retirement age (American Federation of Teachers, 2022). Teachers are more likely to leave schools in higher-poverty communities, serving students of color, and with less desirable workplace conditions, particularly lower compensation and a lack of administrative support (Carver-Thomas & Darling-Hammond, 2019). Too few new teachers are ready to replace them resulting in an ongoing nationwide shortage of teachers (Garcia & Weiss, 2019). This teacher-churn contributes to student learning loss (Sutcher et al., 2019). According to Ronfeldt et al. (2013), "On average, students are harmed by the changing composition in teacher effectiveness that results from teacher turnover, primarily in lower-performing schools" (p. 29). Thus, the more high-quality teachers leave schools, the greater the harm done to vulnerable students. Educational leaders are increasingly challenged to find ways to recruit and retain high-quality teachers.

The loss of teachers in rural schools can be particularly traumatic. In rural settings, a lack of access to services and infrastructure as well as inequitable policies and practices can perpetuate poor academic outcomes and educational experiences for students (Tomlinson, 2019, p. 1). Issues related to a lack of resources, limited access to student services (e.g., physical and mental health) and high-quality childcare, the needs for support among the educator workforce, and barriers to cultivating college readiness are among the most pressing in high-needs rural school communities (Tomlinson, 2019). These challenges contribute to conditions in rural schools that can undermine student engagement and learning (Gurr & Drysdale, 2020) and make recruiting and retaining teachers challenging for educational leaders (Wieczorek & Manard, 2018). During the 2020-2021 school year, nearly 7.3 million students (one in every seven) in the United States were enrolled in rural school districts, defined as rural fringe, rural distant, or rural remote based on the locale code system developed by the National Center for Education Statistics (NCES) (Showalter et al., 2023). By including those who attend a rural school within a district classified as "non-rural" by NCES, the number of students served swells to more than 9.5 million students (one in every five) across the nation (Showalter et al., 2023). High teacher turnover has become a significant educational inequity for students in rural schools.

Educational leaders serving K-12 students and school communities in South Carolina are no exception. Of the 46 counties in the state, 17 are considered rural by all three federal definitions, which include the U.S. Census Bureau; U.S. Department of Agriculture, Economic Research Service; and U.S. Office of Management and Budget (University of South Carolina School of Medicine, n.d.). Notably, 31 counties are considered rural by at least one of these definitions (University of South Carolina School of Medicine, n.d.). Of every 10 schools in South

Carolina, four are in rural areas (Showalter et al., 2023). According to population estimates by the U.S. Census Bureau (2019b), 19.7% of children in South Carolina live in poverty, defined by an annual income of $25,750 or less for a family of four. With a student population of approximately 800,000 (U.S. Census Bureau, 2019b), there are nearly 120,000 students living in poverty in rural areas of the state (Showalter et al., 2023). School districts in South Carolina have among the highest enrollment rates of students of color in the nation (Showalter et al., 2023). The poverty rate for Black children in South Carolina is nearly 2.5 times as high as the rate for their White peers (U.S. Census Bureau, 2019b).

These conditions have myriad impacts on schools in South Carolina, particularly those in rural areas and serving historically marginalized students of diverse backgrounds. For example, rural households in South Carolina have a high mobility rate (lower than only six other states) and the seventh highest rate of households lacking broadband (Showalter et al., 2023). Instructional spending and adjusted teacher salaries in South Carolina are also well below before the U.S. averages (Showalter et al., 2023). Factors such as school climate, teacher salary, and school poverty were strongly correlated with teacher retention rates in South Carolina (Fan et al., 2020), which reflect trends seen across the nation. One in seven teachers in the state did not return to their position after the 2021-2022 school year (The Center for Educator Recruitment, Retention, & Advancement [CERRA], 2022). There were 1,474 vacant teacher positions in South Carolina at the start of the 2022-2023 school year compared to 1,063 the previous year (CERRA, 2022). The increase in teacher turnover is contributing to an ongoing teacher shortage across in the state. While efforts to better understand the factors contributing to the teacher shortage have yielded some recommendations (South Carolina Department of Education, 2023), more research is needed to inform policy and practice.

Reflections on Supervision

Effective supervision, as defined by Glickman et al. (2023), can help school leaders promote collegiality among teachers, placing an emphasis on growth, collaboration, and reflection. Given the detrimental impacts of high teacher turnover, particularly on students in rural schools, research on supervision in rural spaces could potentially increase teacher retention and student learning outcomes. Accordingly, I would like to pose the following questions to scholars in the field of supervision:

- What do we need to better understand about whom supervision serves and how it functions in rural schools?

- To what extent could effective supervision help school leaders recruit teachers to work in rural schools?

- How can supervision help to provide the support needed to increase teacher retention in rural schools?

- How can supervision be used to support early career teachers in rural schools?

- In what ways could more experienced teachers in rural schools use supervision to mentor new teachers, particularly those certified through alterative processes?

- How can we better prepare school leaders to supervise teachers in rural schools?

- How can leaders use technology to enhance supervision, especially in schools where resources may be limited?

- How can leadership coaching be leveraged to develop school leaders as supervisors?

- How can advanced leadership preparation enhance rural school leaders' knowledge of and skills in supervision?

A better understanding of supervision in terms of who it serves and how it functions in rural spaces could help inform leaders' efforts to successfully recruit and retain teachers. With school leaders nationwide facing a growing teacher shortage, research on effective supervision models in rural schools could help leaders in other school contexts recruit and retain teachers as well.

References

American Federation of Teachers. (2022). *Here today, gone tomorrow? What America must do to attract and retain the educators and school staff our students need.* https://www.aft.org/sites/default/files/media/2022/taskforcereport0722.pdf

Carver-Thomas, D., & Darling-Hammond, L. (2019). The trouble with teacher turnover: How teacher attrition affects students and schools. *Education Policy Analysis Archives, 27*(36). http://dx.doi.org/10.14507/epaa.27.3699

Center for Educator Recruitment, Retention, & Advancement. (2021). *South Carolina annual educator supply & demand report.* https://www.cerra.org/uploads/1/7/6/8/17684955/2021-22_supply_demand_report__1_.pdf

Fan, X., Pan, F., Dickenson, T. S., Kunz, G. M., & Hodges, T. E. (2020). *School-level factors associated with teacher retention in South Carolina.* University of South Carolina. https://sc-teacher.org/wp-content/uploads/2020/10/WP-2-Retention_FINAL.pdf

Garcia, E., & Weiss, E. (2019). The teacher shortage is real, large, and growing and worse than we thought. *Economic Policy Institute.* https://files.eric.ed.gov/fulltext/ED598211.pdf

Glickman, C. D., Gordon, S. P., Ross-Gordon, J. M., & Solis, R. D. (2023). *SuperVision and instructional leadership: A developmental approach* (11th ed.). Pearson.

Gurr, D., & Drysdale, L. (2018). Leading high-need schools: Findings from the International School Leadership Development Network. *International Studies in Educational Administration, 46*(1), 147-156.

Ronfeldt, M., Loeb, S., & Wyckoff, J. (2013). How teacher turnover harms student achievement. *American Educational Research Journal, 50*(1), 4–36. https://doi.org/10.3102/0002831212463813

Showalter, D., Hartman, S. L., Eppley, K., Johnson, J., & Klein, B. (2023). *Why rural matters 2023: Centering equity and opportunity.* National Rural Education Association. https://www.nrea.net/why-rural-matters

Showalter, D., Hartman, S. L., Johnson, J., & Klein, B. (2019). *Why rural matters 2018-2019: The time is now.* With the College Board and AASA, the School Superintendents Association. The Rural School Community Trust. http://ruraledu.org/

South Carolina Department of Education. (2023). *Teacher recruitment and retention task force recommendations.* https://ed.sc.gov/newsroom/teacher-recruitment-and-retention-task-force-recommendations/

Sutcher, L., Darling-Hammond, L., & Carver-Thomas, D. (2019). Understanding teacher shortages: An analysis of teacher supply and demand in the United

States. *Education Policy Analysis Archives, 27*(35). http://dx.doi.org/10.14507/epaa.27.3696

Tomlinson, H. B. (2020). Gaining ground on equity for rural schools and communities. In H. B. Tomlinson (Ed.), *Count us in: Advancing equity in rural schools and communities* [Report]. Exploring Equity Issues Series (pp. 1-12). Center for Education Equity, MAEC. https://maec.org/wp-content/uploads/2020/09/CountUsIn-RuralEquityIssues-MAEC.pdf

United States Census Bureau. (2019a). American community survey 1-year estimates. Census reporter profile page for South Carolina. http://censusreporter.org/profiles/04000US45-south-carolina/

United States Census Bureau. (2019b). 2010 census urban and rural classification and urban area criteria. https://www.census.gov/programs-surveys/geography/guidance/geo-areas/urban-rural/2010-urban-rural.html

University of South Carolina School of Medicine. (n.d.). *What is rural?* https://sc.edu/study/colleges_schools/medicine/centers_and_institutes_new/center_for_rural_and_primary_healthcare/what_is_rural/index.php#:~:text=In%20South%20Carolina%20alone%2C%2013,have%20conflicting%20Urban%2DRural%20designation

Wieczorek, D., & Menard, C., (2018). Instructional leadership challenges and practices of novice principals in rural schools. *Journal of Research in Rural Education, 34(*2), 1-21.

Reflections on the Relevance of the Field of Supervision in Education

TRENDS, CHALLENGES, AND CATALYTIC EFFECTS ON PROFESSIONAL GROWTH

Judy Reinhartz

Judy Reinhartz is Professor Emerita at The University of Texas at El Paso where she was a College of Education and University administrator. She was also a professor and administrator at The University of Texas at Arlington, teaching graduate courses in instructional leadership and supervision. She has a Bachelors from Rutgers University, Masters from Seton Hall University, and Ph.D. from the University of New Mexico. Her career has spanned over five decades that have been filled with great diversity and creative experiences much of them focusing on instructional leadership and supervision at all levels to improve academic outcomes. She is the recipient of several awards, including the Chancellor's Outstanding University Teacher Award as well as outstanding contributions to teacher education. She has been a K-12 STEM teacher, staff developer, researcher, member of COPIS that connected her with those well-known in the field, and writer, and consultant. These roles have propelled her enthusiasm for meeting new educational challenges across the country to find collaborative instructional and curricular solutions. As a consultant, an in-person and virtual instructional coach, and a volunteer, she continues to bring the same eagerness to deepen the culture of equity and inquiry among teachers, families, and administrators so that they grow in their pursuit of learning and teaching. Judy is the author of numerous publications, including an article, most recently *Babies, Books, and Math Make Three* and a book, *Growing Language Through Science: Strategies That Work*. Also, she collaborated on a summer virtual library program, *Mathemagical Times*, for K-8 students designed to co-develop math and reading literacy.

Introduction

The year 1977 marked the beginning of my professional career in higher education, having previously been a K-12 classroom teacher. It was a special time, a time when I read scholarly books and articles and had the good fortune to attend conference sessions and meet the giants in the field of supervision. I admired and was inspired by them as I embarked on my own scholarly journey delving into and writing about the theory into practice of supervision and leadership with my late colleague Don B. Beach. That was over three decades ago, and yet I continue to engage in "supervisory activities," often referred to as "coaching" with teachers, principals, and superintendents, employing many of the same approaches and competencies that I used and taught about during my long career. The love of learning and sharing never stopped.

Writing in 1989, Manatt asserts in the Foreword to *Supervision: Focus on Instruction* that the book is timely as America is "… about five years into the latest wave of educational reform" (Beach & Reinhartz, 1989, p. xiii). He continues that there are cycles of reform on average every ten years, stressing excellence and equity as events and economic concerns grab our nation's attention.

Fast forward thirty-five years. His observations hold true with respect to many of the same issues upended by the introduction of technology and social media into our lives and most recently online learning as a consequence of COVID. The public still relies on our schools as the engines to improve the economy and bolster our standing at home and abroad. Looking at supervision through this historical lens will give a perspective on where the field was and is going in the next decades.

The motivation for writing this brief reflection is twofold. One is to return to my roots as a supervisor and professor of instructional supervision. Second is to take a snapshot of the perceptions of supervision and supervision practices in my current work in schools and its impact on student learning vis-à-vis teacher learning. My hope is to demonstrate the instructional power and relevance of supervision and its targeted practices in today's schools and at the same time to convey that the field of supervision continues to be in the forefront of promoting teacher development and student learning.

Historical Perspective

The field of supervision is and has always been multifaceted resting squarely on "the improvement of instruction by fostering the continued professional development of all teachers," including campus and district administrators (Beach & Reinhartz, 1989, p.3). They too have the responsibility of sharing their vision and ideas for moving education forward through teaching.

Others prominent in the field spoke of clinical, self-directed/ focused, cognitive-based, contingency, developmental, differentiated, peer, and instructional supervision each describing their model and emphasizing different approaches to supervision, be it an interactional, eclectic, situational, reflective, individualized, collaborative, and/or instructional all in pursuit of enhancing educators' ongoing learning that benefits students (Goldhammer, 1969; Cogan, 1973; Krajewski, 1976; Glatthorn, 1984; Costa & Garmston, 1984; Glickman, 1985; Beach & Reinhartz, 1989). Many of them supported their models by presenting and describing roles and responsibilities, the need for effective communication, and the abilities to analyze, problem solve, and reflect to offer strategies to address current situations or issues.

Since the emphasis on student academic performance and instructional effectiveness never goes away, it continues to be at the epicenter of educator challenges as well as ongoing research to transform schools. If you accept the thesis that teaching and resultant student learning are key drivers in schools today, then the field of supervision becomes relevant.

But the relevance can emerge only when those in the field recognize and accept that the Pre-K-16 landscape continues to evolve. Equally important is to recognize, what has *not* changed. Research studies over the past century have amassed data on evidence-based best practices. Knowing what effective teaching and learning look like is no mystery (Darling-Hammond, 2021; Darling-Hammond, et al., 2019). Learners at all ages and levels want to be engaged in meaningful experiences, valued, be a contributing member of groups, and have fun both individually and collectively while doing them.

Thus, the key question that remains is how the field of supervision fits into the contemporary teaching-learning dynamic. But before answering this question, terms need to be clarified. There are many ways to define supervision and supervisor. For our purposes supervision is defined as the work that includes the practices and tasks that support teacher development, and those who carry out those functions are called supervisors.

In the 1980s and 1990s different labels such as "early interventionists" responding to personnel needs, as Gallacher (1997) calls them, were used for supervisors. She described these professionals as having the abilities and talents to adapt to a variety of roles, settings, and tasks that required problem solving, divergent and critical thinking in complex environments. These competences, as those described by Gallacher for interventionists, are still essential for supervisors.

Whatever the name of the protocol or model, the end goals that are agreed upon are in support of educators in creating productive and meaningful learning environments for students. Those serving in these support positions today are in dire need for many of the same reasons touted decades ago.

Current Perspective

With "The Coaching of Teaching" in *Educational Leadership* in 1982, the supervision genre expanded (Joyce & Showers). The authors said,

"Like athletes, teachers will put newly learned skills to use—if they are coached" (p. 5). They offered one of the first comparisons of how the coaching process would work with teachers. The authors elaborated on its theoretical basis that involves teaching, practice, and feedback, with the goals of companionship, providing technical assistance, transferring new learning to students using personal facilitation.

If supervision is slowly fading from education, the question is why. There are many negative connotations surrounding the functions and people who carry them out. This image needs to change, to be more user friendly and less top down, directive, threatening, and evaluative. Supervision needs to be viewed as something done *with* teachers, and not *to* them. Perhaps that is why coaching is enjoying a resurgence and a degree of popularity (Bentley, 2020; Lein, 2023; Schembari, 2024).

Supervision is the body of knowledge and practices that makes the difference, not labels. Whether they be instructional supervisors or instructional coaches, their work, purposes, and objectives remain beneficial as they both are tasked with supporting educators in meeting challenges that interfere with promoting effective teaching and learning. These professionals have a lot in common and are integral to the success stories of millions of students, teachers, and families. The value of supervision and supervisors has been and continues to be important to recruiting and retaining educators and to engaging parents in the education of their children.

According to Kraft and Blazer (2018), the current emphasis is on the "individual" rather than on teachers as a group. Growing individual instructional effectiveness takes into consideration the variability of who each teacher is as well as the variabilities of students, parents, and the curriculum. With such an individual perspective, the field of supervision can regain its reputation by focusing on one teacher at a time.

With the increasing demand for teacher effectiveness, promoted most commonly through professional development where all teachers attend the same sessions on the same topics, the results at best have been mixed. Like coaching, the value of supervision lies in the implementation of the principles inherent in the field. Central to both is continuous teacher learning and development.

In recent years, the research on productive coaching has been considerable and has led to the identification of one-on-one mathematics coaching activities to support teacher development (Kochmanski & Cobb, 2023). In examining the work of coaches and in their narrative review of research reports to identify eight one-on-one content-focused coaching practices, the authors found gaps in understanding their effectiveness in modeling instruction, co-teaching, and the specific purposes for engaging teachers in coaching activities (Kochmanski & Cobb, 2022; 2023). The potential for enhancing teacher current knowledge and practices rests, as with other models, on the decisions made, suggestions offered, and questions asked by the coaches in the co-construction of next instructional steps (Gibbons & Cobb, 2017). Addressing these gaps, coaches will be better at clarifying what they need to know to support teacher learning.

Kraft and Blazer (2018) investigated individualized coaching programs that have been implemented with the focus on examining the literature that talks about the "efficacy of teacher coaching as a development tool." "Does one-to-one coaching help teachers get better? If so, how powerful a strategy might this be to improve teacher practice and student outcomes?" (p. 69). Their analysis across sixty studies "found that coaching works," particularly with smaller coaching programs. They assert that there were more positive effects than with traditional professional development approaches and that "the quality of teachers' instruction" did improve "by as much as—or more than—the difference in effectiveness between a novice and a teacher with 5 to 10 years of experience" (p. 70). Once again, this research brings into focus the question of scale.

With headlines from social media, news casts, and newspapers communicating that post COVID students are behind after three years of online learning, there has been renewed interest in the instructional supervision or currently instructional coaching to provide soft as well as technical assistance for educators. Of late, coaching that once focused primarily on teachers is now spreading to others within the hierarchy of the educational community. The notion is that it takes all of us to increase teacher, principal, and superintendent growth.

When reviewing the literature on coaching, it is evident that there are many similarities with the models under the heading of the field of supervision, but what seems to be emerging among all of them are degrees of individuality. Embracing coaching is one teacher-support option that may help to boost supervision as a field of study and reenergize its significance.

From data collected from a small study that included two teacher focus groups of four who participated in the T4T (Teachers For Teachers) coaching project, it was clear from their responses to questions that they gained confidence in their abilities to plan and deliver instruction in ways that contributed to student learning, as evidenced by test scores. As an aside, their yearly evaluations reflected these changes as well. The project was initiated by a volunteer group of retired teachers and professors who implemented it with the endorsement of individual school administrators. As "coaches," our role was not evaluative, but rather one of support for new and experienced teachers in different content or grade level assignments. All coaches participating in the T4T project received a guide, and they attended an orientation where the underlying instructional supervision principles and strategies were presented. The goal was to have a degree of consistency across coaches and the coaching protocol when meeting, observing classroom instruction, and conferencing with teachers, creating a culture of reflective practices. There were regular follow up sessions for coaches throughout the year to debrief and to offer support to each other. Considerable time was spent talking with teachers about goal-setting and action-planning (Reinhartz, 2017; 2020).

As evident in the T4T project, supervision has morphed into different forms of coaching as the primary mechanism for practitioners to support teacher professional development. In fact, it has become one of the fastest growing job-embedded teacher supports, particularly in mathematics and literacy (Darling-Hammond, et. el., 2009; Rodriguez, Abrego, & Rubin (2014; Campbell & Malkus (2011); Cantrell & Hughes (2008).

But as pointed out by Gibbons & Cobb (2017) and others, the coaching literature is scant on providing specific guidance regarding the learning activities that coaches use with teachers. When working with teachers, their study aimed to identify "potential productive coaching activities." The authors identified fifteen of these that were done with individuals (e.g., observing and providing feedback, modeling instruction, and co-teaching) and groups of teachers (e.g., conducting classroom visits; analyzing student test data, classroom behaviors, student work, and classroom videos; and mapping the standards).

This list looks very familiar. In my work with teachers in the recent past in both the T4T project and in the MathAmigos mathematics-literacy coaching, I used the supervision practices with them that I implemented and taught decades ago. It was easy for me to determine the "coaching" activities" that I needed. My point is that even though I was part of programs that were called "teacher coaching," many of the activities uncovered by Gibbons and Cobb (2017) in their study were and are those integral to the field of supervision.

Concluding Reflections

It is evident from this brief chronology that the field of supervision has had a long and productive history that has spawned multiple approaches to target and promote specific teacher competencies and practices. But whatever we call supervision, instructional improvement is central. The similarities between high quality coaching and instructional supervision are obvious. Both require ongoing learning, integrating new practices within existing frameworks as individuals and as team members, experiencing both successes and failures, and analyzing and applying new practices as part of a transformative process. The takeaways here are numerous and build on what has historically been successful in the field of supervision.

These are challenging times indeed, but when has it not been challenging for educators. They need support and pathways to address these challenges and to navigate successfully within the constraints that often stand in the way of promoting positive learning outcomes. The answer to the question of what role does the field of supervision play in education is to increase teachers' professionalism and their pedagogical content knowledge, which in turn increases the quality of learning in our schools.

The field of supervision continues to be an umbrella for catalytic change under which there are sets of job-embedded professional development opportunities that come with shared language, goals, structure, and practices to carry out its vision and mission of supporting educators across disciplines, grade levels, and positions. Using an umbrella to symbolize the field of supervision communicates a sense of preparedness and a haven for teachers to become learners while being supported.

What seems to be important is that research continues to study and identify the evidence-based "ambitious and equitable instructional practices" that broaden our understanding of how to support teachers individually and collectively in pursuit of student learning (Franke et al., 2007; Lowell, 2023). For the field to be sustainable, Butler, Burns, and Willey (2023) call for a renewal in supervisory scholarship to "problematize the work of supervision." Colleges of education should take pause and reflect on the lessons learned to date and consider taking these authors' advice and reflect on ways and the resources needed to prepare high quality supervisors to reverse the current trend of the marginalization of the field.

References

Beach, M., & Reinhartz, J. (1989) *Supervision: Focus on instruction*. NY: Harper & Row.

Bentley, A. L. (2020). Implementing an effective instructional coaching program to benefit the teacher as learner. *DigitalCommons@Hamline*. https://digitalcommons. hamline.edu/hse_cp/476, 1-54.

Butler, B. M., Burns, R. W., & Willey, C. (2023). Toward a Renewal of supervisory scholarship and practice in teacher education: A collaborative self-study. *Journal of Educational Supervision*, 6(3), 47-68.

Campbell P. D., & Malkus N. N. (2011). The impact of elementary mathematics coaches on student achievement. *The Elementary School Journal*, 111(3), 430-454. https://doi.org/10.1177/0022487117702579

Cantrell S. C. & Hughes H. K. (2008). Teacher efficacy and content literacy implementation: An exploration of the effects of extended professional development with coaching. *Journal of Literacy Research*, 40(1), 95-127. https://journals. sagepub.com/doi/pdf/10.1080/10862960802070442

Cogan, M. L. (1973). *Clinical supervision*. Boston: Houghton Mifflin.

Costa, A., & Garmston, R. (1994). *Cognitive coaching: Approaching renaissance schools.* Norwood, MA: Christopher Gordon Publishing.

Darling-Hammond, L. (2021). Defining teaching quality around the world. *European Journal of Teacher Education*, 44(3), 295-308. https://doi.org/10.1080/02619768.2021.1919080

Darling-Hammond, L., Flock, L., Cook-Harvey, C., Barron, B., & Osher, D. (2019). Implications for educational practice of the science of learning and development. *Applied Developmental Science*, 24(2), 97-149. https://doi.org/10.1080/10888691.2018.1537791

Darling-Hammond L., Wei R. C., Andree A., Richardson N., & Orphanos S. (2009). *Professional learning in the learning profession: A status report on teacher development in the United States and abroad.* Dallas, TX: National Staff Development Council. https://outlier.uchicago.edu/computerscience/OS4CS/landscapestudy/resources/Darling-Hammond,%20Wei,%20Adnree,%20Richardson%20and%20Orphanos,%202009%20%20(1).pdf

Franke, M. L., Kazemi, E., & Battey, D. (2007). Mathematics teaching and classroom practice. Ed. F. K. Lester, *Second Handbook of Research on mathematics teaching and learning: A project of the national council of teachers of mathematics.* Charlotte: Information Age Publishing.

Gallacher, K.K. (1997). Supervision, Mentoring and Coaching method for supporting personnel development. *Performing personnel preparation in early intervention: issues models and practical strategies.* Baltimore: Paul. H Brookes Publishing. 191-196.

Gibbons, L. K, & Cobb, P. (2017). Focusing on Teacher Learning Opportunities to Identify Potentially Productive Coaching Activities. *Journal of Teacher Education*, 68(4). https://doi.org/10.1177/0022487117702579

Glatthorn, A. A. (1984). *Differentiated supervision.* Alexandria, VA: Association for Supervision and Curriculum Development. Glickman, C. 1985). *Supervision of instruction: A developmental approach.* Boston: Ally and Bacon.

Goldhammer, R. (1969). *Clinical supervision.* New York: Holt, Rinehart & Winston.

Joyce, B., & Showers, B. (1982) The coaching of teaching. *Educational Leadership*, 40)1), 4-10.

Kochmanski, N., & Cobb, P. (2022). Identifying and negotiating productive instructional improvement goals in one-on-one mathematics coaching. *Journal of Teacher Education*, (74)5, 437-450. https://doi.org/10.1177/00224871221143124

Kochmanski, N., & Cobb, P. (2023). Identifying productive one-on-one coaching practices. *Teaching and Teacher Education.* 121(nn). https://doi.org/10.1016/j.tate.2023.104188

Kraft, M. A., & Blazer, D. (2018). Taking teacher coaching to scale: Can personalized training become standard practice? *Education Next*, 18(4), 68-74. https://www.educationnext.org/wp-content/uploads/2022/01/ednext_xviii_4_kraft_blazer.pdf

Krajewski, R. J. (1976). Clinical supervision to facilitate teacher self-improvement. *Journal of Research and Development*, 9, 58-66.

Lein, J. (2022, February 23). How instructional coaches can use co-teaching to support teachers. *Edutopia,* George Lucas Educational Foundation. https://www.edutopia. org/article/how-instructional-coaches-can-use-co-teaching-support-teachers/

Lowell, B. R. (2023). The student hat in professional development: Building epistemic empathy to support teacher learning. *Science Education.* https://doi.org/10.1002/ sce.21848.

Reinhartz, J. (2017). Sharing My Story and Reflections as a Coach to an Elementary and a High School Teachers, T4T Project. In house publishing.

Reinhartz, J. (2020). T4T Coaching Report, 2019-2020. In house publishing. Rodriguez, A. D., Abrego, M. H., & Rubin, R. (2014). Coaching teachers of English language learners. *Reading Horizons: A Journal of Literacy and Language Arts,* 53(2), 63-83. https://scholarworks.wmich.edu/reading_horizons/vol53/iss2/5

Schembari, J. (2024, January 5). Working proactively with an instructional coach. *Edutopia,* George Lucas Educational Foundation. https://www.edutopia.org/article/ working-proactively-instructional-coach

Students Left Out/ Left Behind

EQUATES TO COPIS—EXPAND THINKING/FLEX MUSCLE

A PERSONAL PERSPECTIVE

Leonard A. Valverde

Leonard A. Valverde is professor emeritus at Arizona State University. He has held many roles: starting as a junior high school math teacher, then a math supervisor with the Los Angeles Unified School District, professor of instructional supervision, educational administration and higher education, department chair, College Dean and Vice President of Academic Affairs at the University of Texas, UT San Antonio and ASU. Also, through a U.S. Department of Education grant, he started the Office of Advanced Research in Hispanic Education and later with W.K. Kellogg Foundation funding became the Executive Director of a multi-state Hispanic Border Leadership Institute consortium of school districts, community colleges, and universities in the southwest. His PhD is from Claremont Graduate University. Dr. Valverde was accepted into COPIS when membership first opened, circa 1974.

This piece is dedicated to First COPIS President, Professor Ben M. Harris, The University of Texas at Austin and to the next generation of COPIS members like Dr. Patricia Guerra, Professor, Texas State University.

Preface

" I was young and strong running against the wind. I'm older now, but still running against the wind." Lyrics from an old song during my early years as an assistant professor in the Department of Educational Administration at The University of Texas at Austin. It captures my actions then and now. This opinion paper focuses on two tracks: 1) the substantive aspect of cultural pluralism and 2) how COPIS can be organized to effectively attend to cultural pluralism. Bear in mind this paper is written from a personal perspective. Yet, it incorporates the views provided by other scholars of my time and hopefully that of the emerging professors and the forthcoming generation of COPIS scholars.

Two disclaimers. One, I do not include the bias against young girls in school, teenage girls, or adult women in higher education and in society. However, history shows that many distorted beliefs, like the denial of voting rights, are held against them and place them in disadvantaged circumstances. I leave this focus to more knowledgeable individuals. Two, I have narrowed my discussion of racial and ethnic groups for brevity. That is to say, I point out the Chinese experience, but not other Asian groups; Native Americans instead of the various individual tribes; Mexicans but not other Latino groups. Also keep in mind, racial and ethnic groups are heterogeneous, not homogeneous. However, they have all been mistreated to their disadvantage. Thus, the United States has lost benefits from generations of these racial and ethnic groups. However, be certain that the United States has benefitted greatly by exploiting these groups.

Introduction

It is necessary to start with an historical framework and reach out to the present day. By a summary review, it will be shown that "minority" persons, or better stated, groups of color, have been left out of society and schooling since the beginning of the United States and much later after (1954 Supreme Court ruling) left far behind. Consequently, COPIS needs to continue and expand its efforts and thoughts about cultural pluralism. COPIS cannot treat cultural pluralism as a trend that will be replaced after a decade with another priority. But let me be clear. Not all COPIS members must focus on cultural pluralism. However, when COPIS members address instruction of students, it is imperative they should include students of color in their thinking. Students of color, as well other students who are different from the white middle-class stereotype, are the majority. Hence, these students have assets, not just perceived deficits—that is, they don't fit the traditional "one-suit-fits-all" concept. Cultural elements must be included when designing new methods when teaching these students. In short, cultural cords need to be considered and woven into the programming fabric.

From its beginning, COPIS was founded with the enduring purpose of helping school personnel provide the best and well-suited instruction to all students so they could gain lifelong learning skills. Given that the minority student population is now the majority, and the culturally pluralistic student body will continue to grow, COPIS will have to sustain its primary focus of curriculum and instruction, but through a prism of multicultural education and language development. Again, keep in mind that school curricula and instruction have promoted white student learning, leaving many previous generations of students of color out and behind—and it appears they will now be left out all over again!

An Historical Summary of Evolution and Devolution

Regrettably the past is still the present when it comes to the schooling of non-white students. While the Declaration of Independence states "all men are created equal," this clearly is not and has not been the case. Yet before its writing, Native Americans, African Americans, Latinos, Chinese, and other dark skin people were denied their cultures (the most basic being language). After the formation of the United States, basic civil, political, and economic rights were also not provided to these groups. Then the societal proposition was the melting pot theory, a falsehood based on assimilation. However, assimilation was really acculturation, meaning persons of color had to renounce their culture: language, dress, hair style, and beliefs. In essence become as the white man.

Native American children as young as four years old were removed from their tribes, homes, and parents and were relocated to Indian Boarding Schools. From 1819 to 1969, in 408 schools across 37 states or territories, Bureau of Indian Affairs (BIA) schools were inflicted upon generations of American Indian children who suffered forced assimilation, e.g., cutting of hair, stripped of their traditional clothing, and forbidden to speak their native language. There was rampant physical, sexual and emotional abuse, malnourishment, over-crowding, and disease (Federal Indian Boarding School Initiative, 2023).

Africans brought to North America as slaves had no rights whatsoever. Their conditions were only slightly better after the passage of the Emancipation Act (1860) by President Abraham Lincoln. Even after the 1954 U.S. Supreme Court ruling of *Brown vs. Board of Education, Topeka, Kansas*, improvement was slow in coming. Desegregation by busing was an additional hardship. Progress began during the 1960s. However, because African Americans were still a minority, caution was taken not to infringe on the rights of the white majority. As will be shown below, this "number's game" justification is no longer used since the demographics have reversed.

Latinos in the U.S., particularly the large population of Mexicans in the Southwest and places like Detroit and Chicago, were viewed and dealt with in a manner very similar to that of Native Americans and African Americans. Because of their brown skin and non-English language, they were to be considered inferior and treated as substandard pupils in schools. Due to societal segregation or red-lining, Mexican Americans were enclosed in barrios. Thus, like Blacks, they were segregated in low-income schools that were old, overcrowded, and staffed with teachers who did not speak Spanish or understand the culture. Thus, the rule of "No Spanish spoken on school grounds" was instituted depriving generations of Mexican American students of learning and completing a high school diploma. The drop-out rate was extremely high. The No-Spanish rule also resulted in physical discipline. Corporal punishment was disproportionally high for Mexican Americans. Those strong Chicanos (first-generation Mexicans born in the U. S.) who refused to transform themselves were expelled.

The Chinese experience is best covered in the book, *The Chinese in America* (2003), written by Iris Chang. She informs readers about the 1882 Chinese Exclusion Act and the following quote in her book speaks volumes: "The Caucasian race has a right, considering its superiority of intellectual force and mental vigor, to look down upon every other branch of the human family." Said by a Colorado lawmaker in Congress." (p.131.) The false inferior race theory used once again.

The historical reality is the opposite. The true representation of the past is that racial and ethnic groups have made a significant positive impact on the making of the United States. But the white power-holders have, to a large degree, ignored the profound economic input by racial/ethnic groups in shaping the mosaic of our society in the past and even more so presently.

From Minority to Majority, Yet Exclusion Continues

The big excuse to keep people of color at a disadvantage, excluded from competitive opportunities, was that they were the minority in number and the status of the white majority had to be protected. In short, the majority rules. Now that the numbers have reversed, you don't hear or read of this rationale anymore. Instead, facts are discarded. To underscore this number's game, the following is offered.

In 2021, there were 49.4 million students enrolled in U.S. public K-12 schools. Of these millions, 22.4 percent were whites, 14.1 Hispanics, 7.4 percent blacks, 2.7percent Asian, 2.3 percent two or more races, .5 percent American Indian/Alaskans, and 182,000 Pacific Islanders or a total of 27.2 million students other than whites, or a difference of 4.8 million more students of color than whites. And the projected numbers are in favor of students of color. By the year 2028, a 2 percent increase is expected for students of color (National Center for Educational Statistics, 2022). Hence, teacher preparation programs and in-service education will require a heavy dose of cultural infusion.

Yet American public-school teachers are far less racially and/or ethnically diverse than their students. In a 2017–2018-year report, there were 78 percent white teachers, 7 percent Black teachers, 9 percent Hispanic teachers, 2 percent Asian teachers and 2 percent American Indian Alaskan Native and Pacific Islanders. (Schaeffer, 2021)

Going from the macro level to the micro level reveals an even more profound difference. Large cities will continue to be the future,

55
5

gaining more people because of job opportunities among other factors. Houston Independent School District, (ISD) is one example. There are 274 schools with an enrollment of 187,000 students; of these, 164,800 (86%) are Latino, Black, and Asian. While local control has been the norm via locally elected school board members, the Texas Legislature (2023) has taken over the district and appointed a superintendent to administer it. The new superintendent is not an educator by training. His charge is to bring about systemic change. Keep the Houston ISD in mind, when I write about what COPIS can and should do with regard to promoting cultural pluralism or instructional improvement for students of color as well as redesigning schools for all students.

Culturally pluralistic student bodies will be the norm across the country. Think of Los Angeles, New York City, Miami Dade County, Atlanta, New Orleans, Dallas, San Antonio, San Diego, San Francisco, Philadelphia, Chicago, etc... All of these and more major urban centers are and will be predominately composed of students of color.

Changing Demographics Brings About Regressive Counter-Productive Actions

While the struggle to overcome years of unnecessary discrimination has been hard, progress towards equality was officially declared via the historic 1954 Supreme Court case of *Brown v Board of Education,* but really started in the 1960s. Regrettably after sixty years, it appears that major actions are attempting to reverse this progress. The state-level, white power structure that controls state education has tried, with some recent success, to backtrack the forward movement of Blacks, Native American Indians, Latinos, and other groups. I provide the most prominent examples.

> In Florida, the teaching of Black history is being prohibited in schools.
>
> In New Mexico, "It's been five years since a New Mexico judge issued a landmark ruling finding that the state was falling short in providing an adequate

education to Native American students…" (Bryan, Associated Press, 2023)

In Arizona, the State Superintendent of Public Education, a non-educator, is attempting to remove Bilingual Education for English Language Learners. The legislature in Arizona (and other states) is removing public funds from school districts and redirecting funds to mostly high in-come parents who elect to send their children to private and parochial schools. The amount of funds, called vouchers, per child ($7,000) does not cover the annual cost of private schools. Thus, only high-income families are able to participate at a now reduced cost, while low-income families have to find additional funds to participate, including transportation to schools. According to Arizona Department of Education, approximately 75 percent of 2023 applicants were children who were not in public schools and received vouchers the year before (Fischer, 6/22/2023). This year it is estimated that vouchers in the total amount of $377.1 million will be taken from the state public education formula funds. In 2019, the amount was $97.1 million (Common Sense Institute, 2023). All of these negatives are being done when the Arizona Latino population is growing, now at 33 percent of the state's population.

As noted above, the Texas State Board of Education has removed local control of the Houston ISD.

At the national level, the Republicans in Congress have stated they want to do away with the Department of Education. Think of the millions of dollars that will be lost to culturally pluralistic students whose school districts rely on ESEA funds, if federal dollars are eliminated due to the removal of U.S. Education Department. As a reminder, the federal department was established during the Presidency of Jimmy Carter.

Before closing this section, let me point out another regressive and most harmful event taking place. The removal of books from public schools. In Florida, it's the removal of Black history; in Texas and Arkansas books can be removed for different reasons, none of which have substance. But clearly book banning will distort the historical record of people of color. White people will have a distorted view. Two books emphasize the facts regarding the contribution by Mexicans and their ancestors in the creation of a vibrant Southwest economy. In the book *North from Mexico*, Carey McWilliams (1968) states "irrigation resulted in economic growth of the southwest" (p. 175). Furthermore, labor-intensive work cultivated and harvested fruit and vegetable crops. As he states "There is not a single crop in the production and harvesting of which Mexicans have not played a major role" (p. 177). He further asserts, "Large planters welcomed Mexican immigrants as they would welcome fresh arrivals from the Congo, without a thought of social and political embarrassment" (p.179). Recall that Cotton was king in the Southern States due to slavery. In another book, *Among the Valiant: Mexican Americans in WWII and Korea*, Paul Morin (1966) shares background information about the 17 infantrymen who were awarded the Congressional Medal of Honor. These books and others paint a much different and fuller portrait of the contributions that groups of color have made in the building of today's American way of life.

What Can COPIS Do To Solidify Effective Education for Students of Color?

A big picture reminder is seen by many scholars. The 21st Century is upon the U.S. and the world. By examining the demographics, it is clear to see pluralism is here and will continue to expand. Population migration is on the rise. People are moving to countries outside their original homelands. Southern and Central Americans are moving through Mexico to North America, mostly to the United States. Eastern and Southern Europeans are moving to Northern and Western Europe. Africa is no different. Birth rates of non-white people are outnumbering that of whites. White death rates are greater than people of color. Life expectancy is longer in years for ethnic and racial groups than for whites. What do these facts mean to the U.S.? If the U.S.A. wants to remain a world leader, it will have to change its educational system and discard unwarranted beliefs in order to produce a smarter pluralistic student body which is the future generation of citizens. Dysfunctional curricula and instruction will need to be eliminated in order to provide a workforce capable of building a strong and vibrant society. We are a vast nation with numerous cultural currents or better stated with a number of cross currents.

Before sharing some specific suggestions for new activities, a few general comments are appropriate. While what I am suggesting may appear to be out-of-bounds for academics and scholars or not the normal professional association activities, keep in mind that society has moved its boundaries as well. For example, the development and expansion of technology has brought about banking on-line, purchasing of products and services on-line, driving places by using GPS installed in automobiles, and placing a phone call or texting from almost anywhere and anytime—as long as you have a cell phone. I assume current COPIS members are using these new devices. For sure, universities are adding on-line courses to their programs.

My two general suggestions are directed to empower COPIS to be more purposeful and influential. Both suggestions are connected and fall under the umbrella that academics/scholars must speak truth to power and gather support from advocacy/community groups. The first general recommendation is thinking power to a new audience. The second general recommendation is exercising muscle. By thinking power, COPIS must point out the programs and propositions that have been shown to be counterproductive. Also, COPIS should point out paradigms and constructs that are suited for certain culturally pluralistic students not only to school decision-makers and classroom teachers, but also to new folks, like local and state school board members, elected state legislators as well as central office district staff, like instructional supervisors, curriculum specialists, and others. The second major recommendation is placing muscle to ideas and constructs by COPIS members so they become incorporated into practice in the classroom or applied to culturally pluralistic students. By muscle, I mean COPIS should target its knowledge-base to local, state, and national power-brokers and policy-makers. It should also include community groups or advocacy agencies. COPIS is probably attending to these streams to some degree, but let me share some specifics which may enhance its accomplishments. COPIS should:

1.   *Dialogue with department chairs and college deans* to increase the number of professors of instructional supervision or increase the number of supervision courses in the degree programs for principals, central office or district-wide directors of programs, and superintendents.

2.   *Establish a formal link with teacher preparation programs* to introduce subject matter that is suited to culturally-pluralistic student bodies.

3.   *Set up two new separate speaker sessions at its annual meeting.* One large open session for future teachers and administrators to attend. The topic to be centered on should have some relationship to cultural pluralism. Another large session for current local policy-makers and practitioners would focus on ideas, programs, and constructs favorable to students of color. Invite the local press to have an education writer publish a story on both open sessions.

4.   *Hold a social event* where COPIS members mingle with invited local leaders (superintendents, school board members, state department officials). Invite leaders of local or statewide advocacy groups. Two examples are: Stand for Children in Arizona and Community Change in Alabama. I'm certain that there are other similar community advocacy groups in other states.

5.   *Encourage and assist COPIS members to hold one meeting within their local region or state.* At this mini COPIS meeting, invite influentials inside and outside of education (business leaders and community groups) those who have a role in what is decided locally or state-wide. COPIS to provide some financial support. See recommendation #7 below.

6.   *Form a standing committee* that will monitor state education issues and provide a report at its annual meeting or by electronic media for group discussion and possible recommendations and actions.

7. *Move to gain more financial resources.* It will require more monetary funds if it is going to expand its reach to other sectors or undertake new activities. As an example of where it might look for additional resources, I offer the following. The Salt River Project, commonly known as SRP in Maricopa County, Arizona, is a power company that serves the greater Phoenix area. SRP annually gives funds to various organizations to support their efforts. SRP is doing so this year by stating, "SRP Cares is proud to support organizations and programs that are committed to advocating for tomorrow's teachers and education programs" (AZ PBS, 2023). I believe other states have agencies or companies such as banks that offer the same type of assistance.

8. *Maintain its social component.* What made COPIS cohesive and agreeable in thought was its ability for members to communicate with each other on a personal level. By getting to know members as individuals with their likes and dislikes, different views were expressed and discussed without malice or causing heated disagreement. Making connections allowed for constructive thoughts. One personal memory may reinforce my point. When COPIS was a very young association, I remember expressing a position that the lines between COPIS and ASCD should be blurred. Professor Robert Alfonso, a senior and nationally esteemed member, responded by saying that lines of difference should be sharpened. He did not try to embarrass me or try to portray me as a young inexperienced assistant professor. His response was viewed as a counterpoint. He accepted me as a colleague with a different position, as did the other COPIS members. As a result, the members benefited from our two different stated positions.

The above recommendations should be discussed as to their feasibility, timing, members' interest, estimated amount of effort, cost, impact, etc. But I stress that COPIS can be the promise, and even though its membership is small, it can be BOLD in thinking and ASSERTIVE in action. The foundation is solid, please build upon it.

Post Script

I end with some closing personal comments. If my perspective reads too much like a political commentary, so be it. I have no regrets. During my teaching of courses and administering, I refrained from speaking about current political events while in the classroom. I became a member of COPIS because it was a vehicle to produce change in schools and hopefully in society as well. My PhD while in education, was designed to prepare persons as change agents. COPIS was one stream dedicated to improving instruction and alter thinking of teachers, administrators, and professors. I believe because of the current and ongoing political right-wing actions and thinking by out-of-date conservatives, COPIS is more important now than ever before. We as a nation of educators are at an infraction point. Shall we move backward to separation and exclusion or will we continue to move forward so that future generations of U.S. citizens contribute mightily to create a much better future.

I end with a point of personal privilege. I thank the following founding members of COPIS for their kindness, assistance, and support both on a professional and a personal basis. May their spirits continue with current and new members –

- Robert Alfonso
- Bob Anderson
- Leslee Bishop
- Ray Bruce
- Jerry Firth
- Noreen Garman
- Edith Grimsley
- Ben Harris
- Helen Hazi
- Richard Neville
- Barbara Pavan
- Tom Sergiovanni
- Karolyn Snyder

References

Arizona PBS. (Fall 2023) *Supporting Education, Together.* Phoenix: V.8, Issue 2.

Byrand, Susan Montoya. (2023). *New Mexico AG vows action on educational case.* Associated

Press, Arizona Republic Newspaper.

Chang, Iris. (2003). *The Chinese in America.* New York: Penguin Books.

Common Sense Institute. (2023). Arizona *K-12 Funding and Enrollment Changes Since FY 2019.* Jan. 11, 2023.

A report on Native American Boarding Schools shows their horrors. (2022). Economist. com/United-States/2022/05/14.

Fisher, Howard. (2023). *Most applying for Arizona vouchers already go to private school.* Arizona Republic Newspaper. Phoenix, 6/22/2023.

Gonzales, Daniel. (2023). *How many Latinos live in Arizona?* Arizona Republic Newspaper. Phoenix, 9/26/2023.

Houston Independent School District. (2023). *General Information: General Information: Facts/Figures.*HISD.org.

McWilliams, Carey. (1968). *North From Mexico.* New York, Greenwood Press.

Morin, Paul. (1966). *Among the Valiant: Mexican Americans in WWII and Korea.* Alhambra, CA: Boarden Publishers.

National Center for Educational Statistics. (2023). *Student Enrollment.*

Schaeffer, Katherine. (2021). *America's public school teachers are less racially and ethnically diverse than their students.* Pewesearch.org. /Short reads/2021/12/10.

In Memoriam— Edward Pajak and Democratic Supervision

REQUIEM IN TWO PARTS

Duncan Waite

Duncan Waite is Professor of Education and Community Leadership at Texas State University and editor, the *International Journal of Leadership in* Education. As a critical scholar steeped in anthropology and education, he has examined (and problematized) sociocultural aspects of instructional supervision, leadership, and administration. His book, Rethinking *Instructional Supervision: Notes on its Language and Culture* (Falmer Press, 1995), featured close interactional analysis (CA) of supervision and supervision conferences. Waite's early experience was as a primary schoolteacher (grades 2, 3, 4, and 5) at the American School of Guadalajara (Jalisco, Mexico). He studied with Keith Acheson & Meredith Gall (*Techniques in the Clinical Supervision of Teachers: Inservice and Preservice Applications),* with Harry Wolcott, qualitative methodologist and educational ethnographer (e.g., *The Man in the Principal's Office*), and C.A. Bowers educational philosopher all at The University of Oregon. Waite has been a member of COPIS since 1990.

Part One

I miss Ed Pajak. In addition to his many and profound contributions to the field of supervision (e.g., Firth & Pajak, 1998; Pajak, 1989, 2000, 2003, 2011), he was a "big thinker," drawing from such diverse knowledge fields as sociology, psychology and more, and percolating fresh ideas. He was intrepid and a stalwart of this organization, The Council of Professors of Instructional Supervision (COPIS), the Instructional Supervision and Leadership special interest group (SIG) of the American Educational Research Association (AERA), and the Georgia Association of Curriculum and Instructional Supervision (GACIS) in particular.

Not so much a gatekeeper, he was more of a Walmart greeter to the world of academia and field of supervision scholarship. He welcomed new, more junior scholars and their ideas. I know, because I was one. I was in my last year of doctoral studies at the University of Oregon studying qualitative research methods with Harry Wolcott (e.g., 2003) and clinical supervision with Keith Acheson (Acheson & Gall, 1992) and looking for a job. A job came open at the University of Georgia (UGA), and I applied. I included with my application a copy of the paper I was due to present at the upcoming AERA meetings.[13] It must have caught Pajak's attention, because he called me. Ed Pajak called me! Me, a lowly doctoral student! You can imagine. I was thrilled. He mentioned the position at Georgia. Long story short, I hired on the next fall: Assistant Professor, Department of Curriculum and Supervision, in one of the last remaining departments with supervision in the department name. I worked with those some of you will know: Ray Bruce, Gerry Firth, Carl Glickman, Ed of course, and Jo Blase (née Roberts). Pajak had integrity, and he was inclusive.[14] He invited me to contribute a chapter (Waite, 1998) to the research handbook he and Gerry Firth were putting together (Firth & Pajak, 1998).[15] And when

---

13 I later published the paper, my first academic journal article (Waite, 1992) and adapted it in my first book (Waite, 1995), for which Pajak wrote the foreword.
14 Of all my colleagues in the department, I trusted Ed.
15 I chose or was given the areas/disciplines of sociology and anthropology. The only guideline Pajak gave me was a one hundred (double spaced) page limit. "Yeah, right," I thought, "How could I even write one hundred pages on this topic?" In the end, it came in at ninety-nine pages. It felt like doing another dissertation and so soon on the heels of my doctoral thesis.

Keith Acheson didn't deliver, Pajak asked me to serve as editor of the foundations section of the handbook.

A year after my arrival at Georgia, the dean decided it would be a great idea to merge our department with Educational Administration to create the Department of Educational Leadership. (Educational Leadership was beginning to trend then. That, or the dean wanted to punish those in both departments by forcing us together.)

My relationship with Pajak was not without its problems. A year or so after the merger of the two departments, Ed took over as Chair of the Department of Educational Leadership. He and his longtime friend and college roommate Joseph Blase, who was professor in Educational Administration, had a falling out. I'm not sure if there was a particular precipitating event or if it was because Blase took it upon himself to cause problems for any and all university administrators.

It was about this time that Jo Roberts' husband Harold came to me and asked if it was true that the university was issuing cell phones to faculty. He had found a second cell phone of his wife's at home and told me he suspected she was having an affair. She had told him the university had issued the phone to her. The next professional conference I attended, Joe Blase and Jo Roberts were together. She soon left her husband and moved in with Blase.

I was still untenured at the time, so imagine my anxiety when Jo Roberts cornered me in my office and, closing the door behind her, told me she and Joe were filing a grievance against Pajak. She wanted me to support them and give her information they could use against him. She threatened that if I didn't, my tenure was in jeopardy. I pointblank refused and told Pajak what had happened. Later, I filed my own grievance against the two of them.[16] Included in my grievance was the fact that when I separated from my wife, Jo Roberts colluded with her, sharing information and fabricating stories about me—Roberts to use against me at the university and my estranged wife to use in divorce proceedings. It went so far and was so egregious that Roberts took to

---

16 Carl Glickman can corroborate this point, as he was on the grievance committee at the time. The response I got from the Dean was that the committee had determined that five of the eleven points I grieved were, in fact, grieve-able.

tailing me after work to see what I was up to and to find where I was living, all information she passed on to my estranged wife.[17]

Needless to say, the department was toxic. I'm amazed that I got tenured there. Pajak's support was a lifeline. I left soon after.[18] Ed took a job at Johns Hopkins University sometime after I left. He died not too long after.

What's the point of this? What's the link?

Part Two

Ed Pajak left us too soon (August 2017, at the age of only 67).[19] In addition to the wealth of scholarship and the memories Ed left, he left me with a puzzle. The last time I saw Pajak was at one of our professional meetings; AERA I think it was. We were walking down the city street making our way from one session to another talking about this and that. He told me that he'd become disillusioned with educational leadership, as a term and as a concept, after initially embracing it. He had been, after all, the Chair of the Department of Educational Leadership at the University of Georgia. He never did tell me why exactly, or if he did, I can't recall now. His dissatisfaction sprung from the difference between educational leadership and instructional supervision. I had been engaged in an initiative to update our AERA Instructional Supervision SIG, not without some controversy.[20] Our membership numbers were falling dramatically. This thing called educational leadership was eating our lunch. The changes abroad mirrored the organizational changes at UGA, with instructional supervision being subsumed, maybe subordinated,

---

17 Sally Zepeda can attest to this. Sally, who took my position at UGA when I left, mentioned to me the numerous times how Jo Roberts gloated about tailing me to find out where I was living and what I was up to and that she colluded with my ex-wife by passing her this information.

18 I soon left the University of Georgia after earning tenure. I accepted a position as Director of the Doctoral Program in Educational Leadership at Appalachian State University. Shortly after my arrival there I received a letter from the Acting Dean of the College of Education at the University of Georgia advising me that because I had left the university, they were dropping the grievance, and it was now moot.

19 He died of an inoperable brain aneurism. It's an indication of the man he was, a kind of avant-garde thinker, that, as his wife Diane told me, he listened to Pink Floyd during his time in hospice. Sadly, Diane passed away last year of a heart attack while at home in her kitchen (A. Pajak, personal communication, January 18, 2023).

20 The compromise we eventually settled on, with input from Pajak, Helen Hazi, Steve Gordon, and others was Supervision and Instructional Leadership SIG.

under educational leadership. So, too, was educational administration as a field. Recently my Israeli colleague Izhar Oplatka confided in me that, like me, he'd stopped attending the University Council for Educational Administration (UCEA), but for different reasons (I. Oplatka, personal communication, Sept. 12, 2022). He felt the organization and its annual meeting were more focused on educational leadership and social justice, when he was interested in educational administration. "Where," he asked, "do you find consideration of administrative tasks and topics such as finance, budget, physical plant, union and labor relations, etcetera?" He began attending other conferences. Me, I stopped going to UCEA, because though I agreed with Oplatka about it being more social justice and educational leadership focused, I felt there was too deep of a managerialist (i.e., administrative) tenor or sensibility running through the conference. Most of the attendees were or had been administrators at one time (principals, central office administrators, university administrators), and despite perhaps acquiring a veneer of progressivism, their ontoepistemology showed traces of managerialism, even neoliberalism, consciously or unconsciously: problems were to be managed, framed in managerialist terms.[21] Pajak and I shared an interest in Willard Waller's (1932) seminal work *The Sociology of Teaching*, especially his chapter on "What Teaching Does to the Teacher." Each of us used that chapter in our work. Pajak (2012) re-examined the original through a psychoanalytic lens using Ovid's myth of Narcissus. I extrapolated Waller's work in examinations of what school administration does to administrators (Waite, 2022). Working as an administrator fundamentally affects the person. It can't not.

Pajak always had teachers at heart. He was a middle school teacher before taking his terminal degree and a university faculty position, but to my knowledge, he was never a school administrator, never a school principal. This, I believe, is why he favored supervision.[22] Afterall, h titled the book he published with the Association for Curriculum and Supervision (ASCD) *Honoring Diverse Teaching Styles* (Pajak, 2003).

---

21 I wrote about this in "'The Paradigm Wars' in Educational Administration: An Attempt at Transcendence" (Waite, 2002).

22 We could rehash the debates about supervision versus administration here (cf. Oliva, 1976; Oliva & Pawlas, 1997), but supervision versus educational leadership is the more crucial question at this particular historical moment, and the point of this essay.

Or perhaps Pajak's discomfiture with leadership was influenced by his reading Hannah Arendt, arguably the preeminent public intellectual of the 1950s and 1960s. It's reasonable to assume that Pajak was familiar with Arendt's (1958) work and how she drew attention to the etymology of leader/leadership in the Greek *archein*: "'to begin,' 'to lead,' finally 'to rule'" (p. 189). This, nested in her discussion of action. The ruler, the leader, commands and his subjects obey and execute those commands. Ruler and leader are synonymous in *archein*.

Pajak (1989) made much of the fact that administrators exercised line authority and supervisors staff "authority"; meaning administrators drew on the power of their position in the organization, but supervisors depended on other means of influence. Supervisors could not command. Teachers are not subordinate to supervisors.[23] Perhaps Pajak was influenced by Arendt's (1959/2000) work on authority and authoritarianism. Arendt wrote:

> authority always demands obedience .... Yet
> authority precludes the use of external means of
> coercion; where force is used, authority has failed.
> Authority...is incompatible with persuasion, which
> presupposes equality and works through a process
> of argumentation.... Against the egalitarian order of
> persuasion stands the authoritarian order, which is
> always hierarchical.... (The authoritarian relation
> between the one who commands and the one who obeys
> rests neither on common reason nor on the power of the
> one who commands; what they have in common is the
> hierarchy itself, whose rightness and legitimacy both
> recognize and where both have their predetermined
> stable place.) (p. 463)

This I believe is the crux of the disenchantment Pajak had with educational leadership, including even instructional leadership: Leadership is more hierarchical, more authoritarian than supervision.

---

23 Of course, this all becomes more muddled when administrators attempt to supervise. This is one of the reasons various supervision scholars argued for a separation of the functions (Acheson & Gall, 1992; Oliva, 1976).

Attempts have been made to make leadership seem more convivial—transformational leadership, servant leadership, culturally-responsive leadership, social justice leadership. They are all at their core hierarchical, and hence inegalitarian and impositional and, to varying degrees, authoritarian when compared to the best, nondirective supervision, to borrow Glickman's (1981) term.

Acheson (1987), for example, advocated that supervisors act more like a Rogerian therapist in clinical supervision conferences, a decidedly teacher-centered, teacher-driven approach.[24] To diminish the power difference between teacher and supervisor, I (Waite, 1995) have recommended that supervisors use what I termed a null approach in classroom observations ("visits," in Franseth's [1955] terms) and dialogic practices in discussions with teachers. The null technique produces no data as such. This frees the supervisor or classroom observer to be more fully present, approximating what the Quakers refer to as witnessing.[25] The lack of data in the supervision post-observation conference means the supervisor's observations can't rest on the presumed legitimacy of "hard data," which itself encourages both the supervisor and teacher to recognize that their analysis or interpretation of the teaching episode is generated from their own particular perspective or standpoint, both spatiotemporal and epistemological, acknowledging that there are numerous (infinite?) such perspectives,[26] each of value and to be respected. And while each perspective-based analysis of the teaching episode both were a part of is respected, they are to be interrogated, which is best done when able to be articulated and made explicit. The resultant supervision conferences can thus go deeper than simply how many girls versus boys the teacher called on, or whether the teacher had the objectives for the lesson posted in the room.

---

24 His advice to us, his students, was to "take data like B. F. Skinner and give feedback like Carl Rodgers" (Acheson, 1987).

25 "Collecting" data while observing is distracting, no matter how good or how experienced the classroom observer. And the more complicated the observation technique, the more cognitive load it demands (Kahneman, 2011); plus, observation techniques or instruments force the observer's focus onto classroom phenomena that may in the end be not that important. Thin or superficial data, produced by using simplistic observation instruments such as checklists, even rubrics, seldom or with great difficulty lead to deep and rich analyses.

26 There may remain issues of insider/outsider knowledge, subjectivities, and what Kahneman (2011) refers to as "the experiencing and the remembering selves."

A yawning chasm separates teachers and administrators. Administrators resent teachers.[27] Teachers distrust administrators, even fear them.

This is as true in K-12 settings as it is in universities. The values of teachers, professors, and administrators differ, as do their aims. Administrators and their staff now make up the majority of university positions, and their proportion is increasing (Graeber, 2018; Waite, 2016; Waite & Swisher, 2017). The numbers and sensibilities of administrators and their staff mean that schools and universities (and hospitals) are "dominated by the professional-managerial classes" (Graeber, 2018, p. 267). Graeber contends that administrators resent teachers, evidencing what he terms "moral envy" (p. 248), because teachers and teaching make a difference; teachers do valuable work, while administrators' work is, in Graeber's terms, bullshit. "Moral envy" is "feelings of envy and resentment directed at another person ... because his or her behavior is seen as upholding a higher moral standard than the envier's own" (p. 248). This explains why teachers are vilified by the public at large, especially when they strike or demand better pay and working conditions, while administrators seldom are: "This can be put down to moral envy. Teachers are seen as people who have ostentatiously put themselves forward as self-sacrificing and public-spirited" (p. 250). Why can't they be satisfied with what they have? Administrators are spared such criticism. Why? Graeber conjectures that even though

> teachers' unions include both teachers and school ad-
> ministrators, the latter being those actually responsi-
> ble for most of the policies most Republican activists
> object to. So why not focus on them? It would have
> been much easier for them to make a case that the
> school administrators are overpaid parasites than that
> teachers are coddled and spoiled. (pp. 250-251)

Though teaching is not a bullshit job (Graeber, 2018), it is suffering increased "bullshitization" (p. 262), where teachers, K-16 and beyond, are tasked with more and more administrative-like "work," which

---

27 Additionally, administrators may feel that teachers are 'inconvenient' (Berlant, 2022).

eats into their teaching and planning time and takes the time teachers could (need to) spend on other aspects of the teaching/caring role not precisely defined as teaching.[28]

Graeber (2018) hypothesizes that many mistakenly equate work with production, usually of material things, such as in the image of a factory worker. This is the ideal economists and policy makers convey in their concept of gross domestic production (GDP) and in analyses that bemoan the number of manufacturing jobs that are being lost. Graeber points to the patriarchal bias of such definitions of work and how they fail to account for caring labor, usually, though not always anymore, done in the household, while "work" is done outside of the household, in factories, plants, and other male-dominated public places. Caring labor is eclipsing factory labor ("production") as the major job type. Caring labor is an essential component of nursing, teaching, nursing homes, and long-term care facilities, and even service jobs such as hair stylist, barista, Uber driver, and even those in financial sectors such as "wealth managers" (Harrington, 2016). In fact, the vast majority of jobs in the new economy have caring labor as a fundamental, if not *the* fundamental, component of the work, though technical knowledge and skills are not unimportant. Seldom are the relational components of most types of work acknowledged in job descriptions, and hardly ever compensated for. Graeber's thesis is that fulfilling, important, and necessary work is undercompensated because of a twisted logic rooted in Puritanism and other theologies which holds that fulfilling work is its own reward and need not be adequately compensated monetarily. This characterizes most care work. Teachers and teaching are the exemplar of this, where the millions of acts of caring and attendant emotional labor often go unnoticed, unacknowledged, taken for granted.

In universities, meaningful and important work is being displaced by bullshit work (paperwork, and other forms of compliance, meetings

---

28 Graeber's (2018) bullshit jobs are of five types or combinations of them—flunky; goon; duct taper; box ticker; and taskmaster (p. 28). All are jobs that even the holders of them describe as worthless (sometimes worse, actually harmful to self or others). He defined a bullshit job as "a form of paid employment that is so completely pointless, unnecessary, or pernicious that even the employee cannot justify its existence even though, as part of the conditions of employment, the employee feels obliged to pretend that this is not the case" (pp. 9-10).

to deal with an increasing amount of bullshit which generate even more of the same), the result of increased corporatization and financialization. The professional-managerial classes have come to dominate the university. The frustration can be felt in one faculty member's comment to the effect that:

> Every dean needs his vice-dean and sub-dean, and each
> of them needs a management team, secretaries, admin
> staff; all of them only there to make it harder for us to
> teach, to research, to carry out the most basic functions
> of our jobs. (anonymous British academic, quoted in
> *The Guardian* as cited in Graeber, pp. 181-182)

Graeber suggested that:

> …if teachers were to rebel they'd have to rebel against
> school administrators who are actually represented,
> in many cases, by the same union. If they protest too
> loudly, they will simply be told they have no choice but
> to accept bullshitization, because the only alternative
> is to surrender to the racist barbarians of the populist
> Right. (p. 269)

The Teaching, The Teacher, The Work, and The Supervision

No one for a second believes the supervision-administration, supervisory-administrator tension (antipathy) was ever resolved satisfactorily. Supervisory tasks were assumed by growing cadres of administrators and administrative staff, or not. The days when "supervision" was in university department names and educators' job titles, when it was a clear, explicit task, function, or role expectation are far behind us. Supervision has morphed and migrated. Some of what we supervision scholars think of as supervision was absorbed into other domains of practice, coaching, for example. Educational leadership occluded the supervision field. Some of what we think of as supervision was grafted onto educational leadership, but not all tasks and functions (roles, processes) survived the change. Those that did, I argue, did so in a radically different form than the original, now forced into a more positivist, corporate capitalist ontology, employed in service of managerialist aims, a tool in the administrators' tool kit.

And the caring aspects of supervision, what of it?

But I think Pajak would agree that though management and administration are foundational to educational leadership they are qualitatively different from instructional supervision.

A Case in Point

Glickman (1990, p. 10) represented his "developmental approach" in a type of flowchart. Reading the graphic from left to right, we find that the "prerequisites" Glickman thought necessary (knowledge, interpersonal skills, technical skills) flow through "SuperVision as Developmental," through one of five "tasks": "direct assistance," "group development," "professional development," "curriculum development," and "action research." These then work through "unification" of "organizational goals" and "teacher needs" to produce "improved student learning" as the product.

Most people, well-established supervision scholars included, fail to catch the feint, the logical sleight of hand which interjects administration and its managerialist ideologies into a formula for supervision, "developmental supervision" (Glickman, 1990) in this case.[29] Most who take up this approach focus on the so-called "tasks," the doing of "developmental supervision"—the direct assistance, group development, professional development, curriculum development, and action research. Or they home in on the "prerequisites" of *knowledge*, interpersonal skills, and *technical skills*.[30]

---

29 It is worth noting here that Glickman served as a school principal before taking up a university position, but, if you recall, Pajak never did.

30 All of the terms and concepts in this schema, but especially those I've highlighted in italics, deserve problematization and examination. So, too, do other aspects of this approach, such as the lack of conceptual integrity of the supervision conference processes (i.e., "directive," "collaborative," and "non-directive"). Funny how all of my students think they are "collaborative." These descriptive terms for conferences are commonsensical and taken on faith, never, to my knowledge, have they been empirically validated. Space and time limitations prohibit a further examination of this approach.

The crux of the issue hinges on what at first glance appears to be the least remarkable feature of Glickman's (1981, 1990) approach. In his schema, mediating organizational goals and teacher needs operates as a kind of conjunction, an operation that joins supervision, its prerequisites and tasks to the "product," which for Glickman is "improved student learning."

Admitting administration and managerialism into the supervision process corrupts and kills it, like a dagger to the heart.[31] Supervisors, those performing supervision in all its manifestations, who, say, are interested in advancing social justice, who believe in democracy and equality step over a line in unreflectively adopting *a* model, any model, not only developmental supervision, and that step takes them further and further away from realizing those admirable goals.

Situational, Organizational Impediments to the Realization of More Democratic Values

We've been aware at least since Weber (1958) of many of the problematic features of organizations (bureaucracies for Weber). Organizations—or the totality of persons, systems (including "culture"), structures, and processes constitutive of them—are conservative (risk-averse), insular, and self-protective. Most institutions are "greedy" (Coser, 1974; Waite, 2022), demanding a certain degree of fealty and acquiescence. Some are greedier still (such as Goffman's [1962] "total institutions"). Organizations, from the most informal association to the more rigid and totalitarian (Arendt, 1968), exact some degree of surrendering of "the self."[32]

---

31 See "Identity, Authority and the Heart of Supervision" (Waite, 2000).
32 Perhaps the most complete surrendering of "the self" is slavery. Historically there have been (and, sadly, still are) different types of slavery, with each party—enslaver and enslaved— having different obligations and responsibilities, and freedoms or their absence (Cox, 1959; Fields & Fields, 2014; Graeber, 2018). Slavery is/was primarily an economic arrangement. The social construction of race and racism in the US arose as ideological justifications of such naked exploitation on a grand scale (Fields & Fields). Graeber (2006) shows how capitalism is rooted in slavery and still bears a resemblance, especially in the wage-labor relations of worker and capitalist: Slaves, he noted: represent precisely what Marx called "abstract labor": what one buys when one buys a slave is the sheer capacity to work, which is also what an employer acquires when he hires a laborer. It's of course this relation of command that causes free people in most societies to see wage labor as analogous to slavery, and hence to try as much as possible to avoid it. (p. 79).

Organizations, institutions, are notoriously undemocratic; that is, if we conceive of democracy and democratic relations as being, foremost, egalitarian. As Rancière (1991) avers, wherever there is sociality there is hierarchy.[33] Furthermore, organizations are abstractions. They are not real. Rancière argued:

> Whatever rationality is given to society is taken from the individuals that make it up. And what is refused to the individual, society can easily take for itself, but it can never give it back to them. This goes for reason as it goes for equality, which is reason's synonym. One must choose to attribute reason to real individuals or to their fictive unity. One must choose between making an unequal society out of equal men [sic]3 and making an equal society out of unequal men. *Whoever has some taste for equality shouldn't hesitate: individuals are real beings, and society a fiction.* It's for real beings that equality has value, not for a fiction. (p. 133, emphasis added)

He added, "One need only learn to be equal men in an unequal society. This is what *being emancipated* means" (p. 133, emphasis in original). The point can hardly be made clearer.

Biesta (2010) reminds us to always think about what the aim of education is. We can extend this and consider what we believe the aim of supervision is. There is no consensus regarding either question. Different people, different groups have different ideas about what education is and should be for—its aim. Some see it as primarily concerned with socialization ("Americanization"), some with workforce preparation and supply, others—I count myself among them—believe the aim of education should be full human flourishing (Wright, 2010), actualization, and emancipation (Lopez, 2020; Waite, 2022). Many

---

33 See Waite (2010, 2022) for a more thorough discussion of hierarchy(/ies), especially in education.

believe that this should be society's purpose or aim (Graeber, 2018; Lawrence, 1950).[34]

So, what might be the aim of supervision? And here we're dealing with definitional distinctions. It matters greatly whether one, for instance, believes supervision should be about raising students' test scores. It matters whether one believes supervision is about school improvement (school, though, is another abstraction). In this case, supervision might be in service of the organization, the school, judging whether students are producing well enough, and judging whether the teachers are. This stance admits more of the administrative surveillance and evaluation function into the supervisor's remit. Surveillance and assessment/judgment impede realization of the teachers' full human flourishing, their emancipation, no matter how well intended, no matter how benign. The evidence for what this system of surveillance and assessment of teachers, of students, does to student flourishing is right before our eyes.

If, as I suggest, education is or should be about human flourishing, then shouldn't supervision be, too? Or be in aid of it? For Rancière (1991 and elsewhere) intellectual emancipation is rooted in equality. For him, equality must be a basic, foundational premise, not some far-off end goal. Education as conventionally realized is and has always been built on unequal relations, as between those Rancière he calls the Old Master and the student and can only result in the student's stultification.[35] This is the only possible outcome from such a relationship—the student's

---

34 D. H. Lawrence (1950) observed: "The living self has one purpose only: to come into its own fullness of being.... But this coming into full, spontaneous being is the most difficult thing of all...

There are two great temptations of the fall of man, the fall from spontaneous, single, pure being, into what we call materialism or automatism or mechanism of the self. *All education must tend against this fall*, and all our efforts in all our life must be to preserve the soul free and spontaneous" (p. 91, emphasis added).

And of society and democracy, he wrote "the first great purpose of Democracy: that each man shall be spontaneously himself—each man himself, each woman herself, without any question of equality or inequality entering in at all; and that no man shall try to determine the being of any other man, or of any other woman" (p. 93).

35 However awkward, "stultification" is Rancière's translator's best option, as she wrote: "In the absence of a precise English equivalent for the French term *abruir* (to render stupid, to treat like a brute), I've translated it as 'stultify.' Stultify carries the connotation of numbing and deadening better than the word 'stupefy,' which implies a sense of wonderment or amazement absent in the French" (K. Ross, in Rancière, 1991, p. 7).

perpetual dependence on the Old Master in an epistemological power-hierarchy. In fact, the whole society is "pedagogicized," individuals dependent on "experts" (Rancière). Biesta's (2010) "learnification" (p. 5)—the oversimplification and bastardization, the reification and commodification of a wild and untamable universal faculty (and right) in a language of learning—directs our attention to the violence visited on what should/could be a transcendental human (and other) capacity for growth, fulfillment, realization, and becoming. Students, each person, become emancipated when they realize the equality of their intelligence and act accordingly. When supervisors serve "the organization," they are complicit in perpetuating its excesses, its injustices, its absorption and devouring of any and all individuals it sees fit to devour, use, and discard.[36]

From its beginning, supervision, especially clinical supervision, has suffered an image problem occasioned by its name and the tensions involved in trying to (re)define itself as something other. To the uninitiated, supervision implies oversight, which in the industrial context or era, and later in the emerging corporate capitalist and neoliberal milieux it implied surveillance and so-called accountability. The corporate capitalist mode of production inveigled supervisors to toe the line and increase productivity, which in schools of the age meant production of ever-rising student test scores. Students were indeed the workers and teachers became middle managers, which meant more and more of what Graeber (2015) called bullshitization of the job—ticking boxes and duct-taping gaping holes in systems. Teachers burned out performing interminable interpretive (Graeber) and emotional labor (Hochschild, 2012), but it is never enough to humanize such a broken and hungry system.

Democracy, or democratic relations, are, first, egalitarian. In my view, and I believe Pajak would've concurred, supervisors were not above or superior to teachers, but equal to. Or, at least, they ought to be. But too many things get in the way. Supervisors are usually given a

---

36 I still recall how horrified and shocked I was when upon his retirement from the University of Oregon, Keith Acheson was made to vacate his university office post haste. One of the most dignified and influential scholars in our field was treated in as undignified a manner as was possible, given the bum's rush. The capstone bit of learning my graduate program afforded me was the lesson that organizations have no soul.

title such as Curriculum Director or whatever. They are plucked from a classroom and relocated elsewhere, distant from teaching and teachers' work. Legion are the cases where those given supervisory roles are alienated from teachers.[37] Social professional distance can be caused by system demands and expectations and those that are self-imposed. Teachers erect barriers. Teachers, too, foist expectations on those who supervise, not all of them conducive to professional working relations. This is the first hurdle (well, actually the second) my supervision students must face and surmount. (The first being their own sense of inadequacy, especially if they are relatively inexperienced and the teacher with whom they are working is a veteran of many years.)

Distance is created as well by how the supervisor comports herself, how she goes about her job.

How does the supervisor see their job? Do they follow a particular supervision model or approach rigidly? What "tools" such as observation techniques do they use?[38] Investment in or ownership of the data the supervisor "produces" puts limits on conference discourse. My null technique for classroom observation is a partial remedy to this as it "produces" no data per se. This lessens the likelihood the supervisor or teacher will reify or objectify what in reality are subjective impressions of teaching episodes witnessed (i.e., "data").

How the conferences proceed affect the power relations between teacher and supervisor. The language each uses provides context cues as to who each thinks they are and what kind of occasion this is. Supervisors are explicitly taught to lead the conferences or perhaps they feel this is their role. Most supervision textbooks encourage it (e.g., Acheson & Gall, 1992). Supervisors are especially keen to lead the conference if they have collected classroom observation data. But such a seemingly innocuous practice as leading off with a question, no matter how well intended, has severe ramifications for who gets to speak, with what authority, and what can get said (Waite, 1995). If the supervisor leads with a question (e.g., "So, what do you think about

---

37 They are like the Education Specialist (EDS) graduate student I had from southern Georgia who said that upon taking her first supervision job, the teacher who taught next door to her for so many years shunned her and ended their friendship forever.

38 I've shown (Waite, 1995, p. 119) how the choices supervisors make can successively narrow the things that get talked about in supervision conferences, in effect silencing the teacher.

the lesson?" or "How do you think the lesson went?") the teacher is culturally primed to respond. The floor reverts to the supervisor who can judge the adequacy of the teacher's response or take the conversation in another direction. This volleying back and forth always leaves the supervisor in control of the conference. Sometimes it's better to avoid asking a question in favor of making a statement instead (Scollon & Scollon, 1986).

Supervisors have become rarer in public education. Where once "supervisor" was a job title (see Oliva, 1976), it no longer is, except in teacher education. Rather than speak of supervisors, we'd be better off thinking of the tasks of supervision (Harris, 1985).[39] Edith Grimsleyonce said that supervision is something which if you don't attend to it, it doesn't get done (E. Grimsley, personal communication, Sept. 20, 1990). [40]Now there are no longer those whose title includes "supervisor" or "supervision." what were formerly the tasks of supervision have dissipated, migrated into other educational domains and positions. Have they disappeared entirely? No, but they've changed drastically. And it matters who is doing what, under what flag the tasks are taken on. Take teacher or classroom observation. The classroom observation done by a principal is qualitatively different than that done by an assistant principal, which is itself qualitatively different than that done by, say, an instructional coach.

It may very well be that if we're to see the type of supervision I'm writing about—egalitarian, democratic supervision—it's best done by someone already equal to (or "below") the hierarchical level of the teacher.[41] Graduate students in a supervision class, other teachers, a coach, student teachers, the teacher's students themselves are likely

---

39 Paradoxical, I know. Maybe hypocritical. Despite writing that it's more honest to think of the tasks of supervision than it is a "supervisor," the convention of writing of "the supervisor" is too convenient to easily dismiss. When I write "supervisor" I intend whomever is performing a supervisory task at the moment, rather than a title or position.

40 It was Edith Grimsley's retirement that created the faculty position I took up at the University of Georgia.

41 This evokes for me the Biblical parable of it being easier for a camel to pass through the eye of a needle than for a rich man to enter the kingdom of heaven. Not that it can't be done, but it's difficult to establish and then maintain co-equal relations (Holloway, 2002), especially given what I've written above about organizations, status, hierarchies, power, personality factors, and more.

candidates. But if an educator wants change, and to change, clinical supervision is an ideal starting place.

Fanning the Embers of Democracy
One Interaction at a Time

Book bans. "Don't say gay" censorship. Bounties for calling out teachers. Students snitching on their teachers. Anti "woke" legislation. Decimation of DEI programs and initiatives. School vouchers. Anti LGBT+ education policies. Anti "CRT" campaigns. These and other efforts by the reactionary Christian Right and ultra-conservative groups and media are chilling free intellectual discourse in primary, secondary, and higher education. Teachers are burning out. Teachers are leaving in droves. Administrators are leaving, retiring, getting fired, or run off. Schools are the front line in the Right's "culture wars" (see Brown, 2019). Even those with no children in school cause a ruckus at school board meetings, threaten teachers and administrators with violence, harass them at their homes. Classrooms and schools are roiling with heated and angry politics. Have schools become no-go zones for free inquiry and honest, truthful discussion? Teachers are fearful, and not just because of more stringent so-called accountability measures. The possibility of school violence preys on teachers constantly.

What can a lowly supervisor who believes in democracy, free expression, and intellectual curiosity do? How can such a supervisor serve a teacher who believes in these core values? What of the teacher's (and supervisor's) coming into being, fulfillment, flourishing, realization? In short, what of emancipation?[42]

Supervisors and those performing supervision must tend to their self-realization, their fulfillment, their coming into being, their emancipation. If not, it's nearly impossible to assist teachers in this. Intellectual emancipation signifies equality (Rancière, 1991), the belief that one is equal to any and all, and acting accordingly. Intellectually emancipated supervisors believe teachers are their equal. If a teacher

---

42 Space prohibits the development of this here. For a longer, more in-depth treatment, see my *On Educational Leadership as Emancipatory Practice: Problems and Promises* (Routledge, 2022). However, as these ideas are ever evolving, some of what I write here may differ from what I wrote there.

doesn't believe they are the supervisor's equal, supervisors can work with them to aid in their emancipation.

Despite the political and micro political environments that are schools, there are moments, spaciotemporal instances, where emancipation can be realized and practiced. A supervision conference can be such a space. Pajak's (1989) distinction between line authority (administrator) and staff authority (supervisor) would suggest that it might be easier for a supervisor to get teachers to see them as equals; more difficult, perhaps, for the administrator—difficult, but not impossible. For the supervisor, thinking they are equal to teachers may be easier than thinking the teacher equal to them. But equality means all are equal. Equality in practice is non-coercive, deliberative, consensual.

In hierarchical organizations (most corporate capitalist organizations) such as schools, realizing equality takes work. Holloway (2010, p. 43) suggests "horizontality" in place of, as a counter to the verticality of hierarchies:

> Horizontality is part of the assertion of our own
> subjectivity, the rejection of vertical structures, chains
> of command which tell us what to do, which make
> us the object of the decision-making of others....The
> idea of horizontality is that all should be involved in
> decision-making processes on an equal basis and that
> there should be no leaders. (p. 43)

And here we come back around to supervision and the problem of leadership, instructional leadership included, and why I believe Ed Pajak was dissatisfied with educational leadership. Holloway notes that horizontality is difficult in practice "since informal patterns of leadership often grow up even where there are no formal structures" (pp. 43-44). It's better, he wrote, and "more helpful to think of horizontality not as an absolute rule but as a constant struggle against verticality" (p. 44).

In a hierarchy, who leads? Who follows? How is it they come to occupy those spaces? Rancière (2010) invoked Plato and his *Republic* to address this question. Plato held there were seven titles that determined who was fit to rule (ruler being synonymous with leader for our purposes).

> Four of them [are]…relating to birth: naturally those
> who are born first or are highborn command. Such is
> the power of parents over their children, the old over
> the young, masters over their slaves, and highborn
> people over men of no account. Then come two other
> principles that also express nature if not birth. First, we
> have "the law of nature"… the power of the strongest
> over the weakest….The sixth title inventoried: the
> power which is accomplished by the law of nature
> properly understood, the authority of those who know
> over those who are ignorant. (pp. 39-40).

As Rancière recounts it, there appears

> …a strange object, a seventh title to occupy the superior
> and inferior positions, a title that is not a title, and that,..
> [Plato] tells us, is nevertheless considered to be the
> most just: the title of that authority that has the "favor
> of heaven and fortune": the choice of the god of chance,
> the drawing of lots, i.e., the democratic procedure by
> which a people of equals decides the distribution of
> places. (p. 40)

He continued:

> All it requires is a throw of the dice. The scandal is
> simply the following: among the titles for governing
> there is one that breaks the chain, a title that refutes
> itself: the seventh title is the absence of title. Such is the
> most profound trouble signified by the word democracy.
> (p. 41)

Among equals each is fit to lead. Why not select a leader by lottery or the throw of a die? The casting of lots provides a safeguard for democracy and democratic relations: "The drawing of lots was the remedy to an evil at once more serious and much more probable than a government full of incompetents: government comprised of a certain competence, that of individuals skilled at taking power through cunning" (p. 42). "Good government," in Rancière's reading of Plato, "is the government of those who do not desire to govern. If there is one category to exclude from the list of those who are capable of governing it is in any case those who set their sights on obtaining power" (p. 43).[43]

Leaders appear out of nowhere and all too many people, educators, too, are ready to lead, to accept a leadership role, to direct others and tell them what to do. We've seen too often how supervision students and veteran supervisors as well are all too eager to tell the teacher with whom they are working what to do (cf. Glickman's "directive supervisory behavior"). We don't stop to think, or perhaps we just don't care, how limiting this is, how obstructive to the teacher's growth and development. Early on, Grimmett and Housego (1983) authored a study whose findings were that the single greatest impediment to a teacher's growth was the supervisor. Sheldon Kopp (1972) wrote *If You Meet the Buddha on the Road, Kill Him!*[44] with a not-dissimilar message: the supervisor's advice is the supervisor's advice, from their subject position and from their framing of the issues and solutions. The growth, especially growth toward self-realization, coming into being, nourishing and fulfillment, has to come from within.

References

Acheson, K. A. (1987). *Class notes.*

Acheson, K., & Gall, M. D. (1992). *Techniques in the clinical supervision of teachers: Preservice and inservice applications (3rd ed.).* Longman.

Arendt, H. (1958). *The human condition (2nd ed.).* The University of Chicago Press.
Arendt, H. (1968). *The origins of totalitarianism.* Harcourt.

Arendt, H. (2000). What is authority? In *The portable Hannah Arendt.* P. Baehr (ed.) (pp. 462- 507). Originally published as Arendt, H. (1959). What was authority? In *Between past and future.* C. Friedrich (ed.). Harvard University Press.

Berlant, L. (2022). *On the inconvenience of other people.* Duke University Press.

Brown, W. (2019). *In the ruins of neoliberalism: The rise of antidemocratic politics in the West.* Columbia University Press.

---

43 Plato's philosopher-king.
44 He's not Buddha. Buddhahood lies within. Kopp's "Eschatological Laundry List" includes "17. There are no great men." And my favorite: "18. If you have a hero, look again: you have diminished yourself in some way" (p. 223).

Coser, L. A. (1974). *Greedy institutions: Patterns of undivided commitment.* The Free Press.

Cox, O. C. (1959). *Caste, class, and race: A study in social dynamics.* Monthly Review Press.

Fields, K. E., & Fields, B. J. (2014). *Racecraft: The soul of inequality in American life.* Verso.

Firth, G. R., & Pajak, E. F. (Eds.) (1998). *Handbook of research on school supervision.* Macmillan

Franseth, J. (1955). *Supervision in rural schools: A report on beliefs and practices.* U.S. Department of Health, Education, and Welfare.

Glickman, C. D. (1981). *Developmental supervision: Alternative practices for helping teachersimprove instruction.* Association of Curriculum and Supervision.

Glickman, C. D. (1990). *Supervision of instruction: A developmental approach (2nd ed.).* Allyn & Bacon.

Goffman, E. (1962). *Asylums: Essays on the social situation of mental patients and other inmates.* Anchor Books.

Graeber, D. (2015). *The utopia of rules: On technology, stupidity, and the secret joys of bureaucracy.* Melville House.

Graeber, D. (2018). *Bullshit jobs: A theory.* Simon & Schuster.

Grimmett, P. P. & Housego, I. E. (1983). Interpersonal relationships in the clinical supervision conference. *The Canadian Administrator, 22*(8), 3-28.

Harrington, B. (2016). *Capital without borders: Wealth managers and the one percent.* Harvard University Press.

Harris, B. M. (1985). *Supervisory behaviors in education* (3rd ed.). Prentice Hall.

Hochschild, A. R. (2012). *The managed heart: Commercialization of human feeling.* University of California Press.

Holloway, J. (2002). *Change the world without taking power: The meaning of revolution today.* Pluto Press.

Kahneman, D. (2011). *Thinking, fast and slow.* Farrar, Straus and Giroux.

Kopp, S. B. (1972). *If you meet the Buddha on the road, kill him!: The pilgrimage of psychotherapy patients.* Bantam Books.

Lawrence, D. H. (1950). *Selected essays.* Penguin Books.

Lopez, A. E. (2020). *Decolonizing educational leadership: Exploring alternative approaches to leading schools.* Palgrave Macmillan.

Oliva, P. F. (1976). *Supervision for today's schools.* Crowell.

Oliva, P. F., & Pawlas, G. E. (1997). *Supervision for today's schools (5th ed.).* Longman.

Pajak, E. F. (1989). *The central office supervisor of curriculum and instruction: Setting the stage for success.* Allyn & Bacon.

Pajak, E. F. (2000). *Approaches to clinical supervision*. Christopher-Gordon Publishers.

Pajak, E. F. (2003). *Honoring diverse teaching styles: A guide for supervisors*. Association for Curriculum and Supervision.

Pajak, E. F. (2011). Cultural narcissism and education reform. *Teachers College Record, 113*(9), 2018-2046.

Pajak, E. F. (2012). Willard Waller's *Sociology of Teaching* Reconsidered: "What does teaching do to teachers?". *American Educational Research Journal, 49*(6), 1182-1213.

Rancière, J. (1991). *The ignorant schoolmaster: Five lessons in intellectual emancipation*. K. Ross (trans.). Stanford University Press.

Rancière, J. (2014). *Hated of democracy*. S. Corcoran (trans.). Verso.

Scollon, R., & Scollon, S. (1986). *Responsive communication: Patterns for making sense*. Black Current Press.

Waite, D. (1992). The instructional supervisor as a cultural guide. *Urban Education, 25*(4), 423- 440.

Waite, D. (1995). *Rethinking instructional supervision: Notes on its language and culture*. The Falmer Press.

Waite, D. (1998). Anthropology, sociology, and supervision. In G. R. Firth & E. Pajak (eds.), *Handbook of research in school supervision* (pp. 287-309). MacMillan.

Waite, D. (2016). Whistling past the graveyard of our own demise: How neoliberalism, corruption, status hierarchies and The Imperium threaten higher education. In A.Stachowicz-Stanusch & G. Mangia (eds.), *The dark sides of business and higher education management*, Vol II. (pp. 83-113). Business Expert Press.

Waite, D. (2000). Identity, authority, and the heart of supervision. *International Journal of Educational Reform, 9*(4), 282-291.

Waite, D. (2002). 'The Paradigm Wars' in educational administration: An attempt at transcendence. *International Studies in Educational Administration, 30*(1), 66-81.

Waite, D. (2010). On the shortcomings of our organizational forms: With implications foreducational change and school improvement. *School Leadership & Management, 30*(3), 225-248.

Waite, D. (2022). *On educational leadership as emancipatory practice: Problems and promises*. Routledge.

Waite, D., & Swisher, J. (2017). Merrily digging our own graves: Teachers and administrators, their work lives and relationships within emerging working conditions. *Education and Society, 35*, 63-86.

Weber, M. (1958). *The protestant ethic and the spirit of capitalism*. T. Parsons (trans.). Scribner. Wolcott, H. F. (2003). *The man in the principal's office: An ethnography*. AltaMira Press.

Wright, E. O. (2010). *Envisioning real utopias*. Verso.

AFTERWORDS

Reflections on the Think Pieces

Think Piece Reflections from a Practitioner Lens

Jennifer Lane

 Jennifer Lane has served as a K12 practitioner for the past 14 years with roles spanning from teacher to instructional coach, to district level administrator. She is currently serving as Director of Curriculum and Instruction at Lindale Independent School District in Lindale, Texas. Through this role she has led her district in Teacher Incentive Allotment local program implementation and successful designations, district instruction and assessment alignment, ongoing professional development experiences shifted to align with the principles of andragogy, and instructional supervision and coaching among many other projects.

Jennifer is also a doctoral student in the School Improvement focused Educational Doctorate program at the University of Texas at Tyler with expected graduation in August 2024. Her dissertation titled, Investigating the Impact of Teacher-Led English as a Second Language (ESL) Intervention and Computer Assisted Language Learning (CALL) on Second Language Acquisition, is scheduled for defense in June 2024. Throughout her time as a graduate student, Jennifer has had the opportunity to experience higher education as an adjunct professor for preservice teaching skills courses, and has had the unique experience of participating in the iSEE Belize project training teachers and supervisors with the Ministry of Education in Belize.

> Throughout these experiences, Jennifer has been immersed in the world of instructional supervision locally, at the higher education level, and globally. These opportunities were almost all exclusively made possible by Dr. Yanira Oliveras, whom she proudly studies under and invited her for admission into COPIS two years ago.

I am deeply honored to be asked to provide my reflections and musings regarding instructional supervision and the pieces submitted by COPIS scholars. Surrounded by the talent of those within the COPIS group, I often feel like a microscopic amoeba in a vast ocean of giant majestic sea creatures, but I am always guaranteed to leave with a deeper understanding for instructional supervision and a rejuvenated passion for this profession. My approach to reflecting on the collection of think pieces was to simply enjoy reading, take it all in, and listen acutely to every reaction in my brain to let my thoughts for the panel take shape, all while hoping something of value would surface.

As it turns out, one of my very first metacognitive noticings showed itself as an undercurrent in nearly every think piece, which was dually vindicating and fascinating for me. Collectively, you all have confirmed the dissonance I have been feeling, equipped me with a visual metaphor to clarify my experiences, and provided several interesting and exciting potential solutions. As someone with one foot firmly planted in the field and the other foot in higher education and scholarly study, I often feel like I am doing splits despite the positive advancements on both sides. After reading the think pieces, it seems that I am not the only one feeling the stretch.

The Dissonance

A nagging dissonance kept creeping in while reading the pieces highlighting the journey from evaluation to supervision and the depth and complexity of that transformation. All I could think about was that the practitioner culture, unfortunately, has not shifted along with it, but rather continues to "wallow in a quagmire of confusion" as Glanz mentioned. While I understand that my perspective is phenomenologically constructed from my lived experiences and that no two realities are the same, I have been involved with multiple K-12 settings fulfilling many different roles across state lines, and my experiences have been similar. There seems to be a strong culture of oppositional defiance among practitioners when it comes to anything mandated at any level and a strong societal pressure within the educational field to conform to this behavior—especially as it relates to the "initiation" of new teachers. This foundational mistrust and oppositional defiance in the field is mentioned in Hazi's piece regarding the "crisis of mistrust" which delineates the various levels and layers of this perception inside and outside of educational systems and is also discussed within the global confines of terminology misconceptions in the piece from Oliveras.

I have also recognized examples to support this mistrust throughout my time in the field. One example is the Texas Teacher Evaluation and Support System, the method of teacher appraisal mandated in Texas. Instead of looking at something that is mandated with the idea that since it must be done, it should be done most beneficially, it is treated as an inconvenient administrative task more often than it is embraced as an opportunity for mutual growth. Hazi mentioned this complex dynamic by noting the difficulty of true instructional supervision when the same individual is responsible for evaluation and mandated to do so. This is compounded with initiatives like the Teacher Incentive Allotment program and its appraisal component, tying supervision to life-changing incentive pay for teachers creating a culture of instructional supervision infidelity for administrative and incentive check boxes.

It also seems there is a strong wall put up against anyone who is not currently in the classroom. It is common to experience a disregard for advanced degrees and scholarly research due to the belief that unless someone is on the "frontlines" they cannot possibly be an expert in the field. Although I do believe there is some credence to that attitude and justification for how that belief came about, even if there were not, we know perception is reality, so we have a responsibility to explore these perceptions and perspectives of practitioners. I believe it would be beneficial to lean more into the "why" behind this collective mistrust and oppositional viewpoint, to bridge that gap and begin the work of repairing that perception.

The "Why" From a Practitioner Lens

Perhaps one of the biggest contributors to mistrust and oppositional defiance is the weight of accountability expectations. I have seen many educational leaders struggle to juggle the weight of state and federal expectations and adjust many of their systems and processes with the sole goal of increasing accountability above anything else. Hazi supported this in her piece, saying "teacher evaluation also has so many regulations and legal mandates that make it dysfunctional and resistant to fixing." Another contributing factor specifically lies in the complexities of the various campus and district settings. My experiences with rural districts have all confirmed that within those settings, principals are typically expected to be the instructional leaders, the project managers, the evaluators, the instructional coaches, managers of people, accountability experts, student behavior technicians, campus policymakers, extreme organizers, and so much more. This makes it impossible to engage with instructional supervision in the way that it needs to function to yield successful growth and improvement. This was supported by Paufler's piece in her narrative on rural settings and their specific challenges. Some settings are battling a "good is the enemy of great mentality." For example, the setting I am currently in has historically received the highest marks and ratings with the state accountability system, resulting in a culture that is fearful of change lest that change bring down what accountability says is working, contributing to an even bigger wall against anyone outside of the campus or classroom and their potential expertise.

One of the hardest things for me has been learning about all this great information regarding the science of school improvement and instructional supervision and then feeling like Sisyphus when trying to implement these seemingly simple tools in practice. As I have struggled with this internally for the past few years, the think pieces have helped me to understand that what we need to be asking is what role we play in shifting the practitioner culture to catch up with the growth of instructional supervision. How do we help practitioners shift OUT of the oppositional defiance that comes from a deeply rooted mistrust in educational leaders, policy, and supervision? We must look closer at the qualitative practical perception data of the collective experiences of practitioners to begin this work of reparation.

Extending the Umbrella Metaphor

Reinhartz likened instructional supervision to an umbrella in her piece. This visual metaphor helped explain my collective dissonance. An umbrella, like instructional supervision, is a tool to help make traveling from point A to point B easier when outside conditions are not ideal. Society as a whole has a basic understanding of what an umbrella is, and what function it serves. If carried with you, it can be a great source of aid and comfort in unexpected weather. I also love that instructional supervision can be viewed as an umbrella topic, with many other areas of focus and fields impacted under its shelter. Extending this metaphor to include practitioner implications helps to illustrate my lived experiences. In the field, I have seen many practitioners who do not believe in the use of an umbrella, as they do not see or acknowledge there will be a storm. No one wants the seemingly extra thing to carry if they do not see the rain clouds for themselves. Many practitioners would rather make an uncalculated dash for it instead of fussing with the up and down of an umbrella. Many practitioners prefer to sit stationary, stuck, while they wait for the rain to end, as they believe it is only a matter of time before "this too shall pass." I have seen the peer pressure involved with supportive tools, such as it is not cool to be seen carrying an umbrella, and you are somehow weaker if you choose to use that shelter instead of making a run for it. Many educational leaders feel they do not have time to teach others how to use an umbrella, or simply cannot fit the umbrellas they need to pass out to others in their already full bags.

In the world of umbrellas, umbrella companies would not attempt to get more consumers to buy and use umbrellas by getting politicians to pass a law mandating that every citizen is required to carry one. Nor would they simply bring the umbrella back to a lab in isolation and try to figure out solutions independently. What they would do, and have done, is change the design of the umbrellas to make them more compact and accessible, improve the function and marketing, and most importantly, try to make umbrellas more attractive to consumers.

Case in point is the clear umbrella that became popular, different sizes, colors, and patterns emerged as well. Most recently, the umbrella has been reengineered to be inverted, drastically improving the ease of use and access, increasing both the purchase of the umbrella and its use. All these changes were made through market research and by seeking out those who hate umbrellas and collecting feedback to inform and change the way umbrella experts approached the design.

I believe that this is exactly what is needed with instructional supervision. The evolution of instructional supervision has come a long way, but the perception surrounding it has not. Instead of mandating instructional supervision or staying in the scholarly lab to continue studying it as a construct, we need to shift focus into studying those that are resistant to it. We need to begin market research to better understand the consumers.

Proximity as a Solution

The COPIS scholars overwhelmingly agreed with the idea of turning our time, attention, and efforts to proximity in the field and to practitioners. The Personal Reflections piece asserted that because instructional supervision is implementation science, its scholars must remain close to practitioners. Glanz noted the critical importance of focusing on the instructional core, which means focusing our attention on the inside of the classroom where the work takes place. This was echoed by Reinhartz and the idea of keeping instructional improvement the focus of this work. Buchanan explored the concept of instructional supervision as an edge community to bridge teacher education and educational leadership, pointing to an exciting opportunity for positions like teacher preparation faculty and field supervisors. The hope within these edge opportunities would be to build relationships with seasoned teachers and campus leaders through the preservice students placed in their classrooms to work toward positive improvement. Glickman's colleague noted the conclusion that teachers should be involved in the design and implementation of educational research, and Johnson noted that "instructional supervision has a duty to stay on top of the current state of instructional practices and the state of students entering the classroom." Paufler suggested better preparation of educational leaders to build the capacity of leading instructional supervision work within the proximity of classrooms. Piantanida explored the importance of inviting other stakeholders, fields, and layers of those affected by this work for improved global understanding and adjustments for improvement of practitioner perception.

It was very clear to me after reading this think piece collection, that we all seem to be feeling and acknowledging the dissonance between the improved understanding of instructional supervision, and the stall it is experiencing in implementation due to practitioner perceptions and mistrust. It was also clear to me that we all seem to be feeling pulled into the field to close those gaps and help heal those negative perceptions. I am most excited about the discourse of getting higher education scholars into the field and getting teachers into scholarly conversation, as that might clarify terminology while lessening some of the collective mistrust. I look forward to seeing more of the efforts toward closing the gaps, getting into practitioner spaces, and the practitioner market research that is sure to come from COPIS. I hope I can be a positive and impactful conduit of this work moving forward as well.

Reflections from the Sidelines of Supervision

Maria Piantanida

Maria Piantanida, PhD graduated in 1982 from what was then the University of Pittsburgh's Department of Curriculum and Supervision. She served as the Director of the newly created Department of Hospital-wide Education at Allegheny General Hospital and subsequently served as a curriculum consultant on a number of projects related to education in the health professions. As an Adjunct Associate Professor at the University of Pittsburgh, she taught courses on qualitative inquiry in the School of Education. As an Adjunct Associate Professor at Carlow University, she has taught creative inquiry to Masters students and will be teaching in Carlow's new EdD program. She is the co-author of On Being a Scholar-Practitioner: Practical Wisdom in Action and *From Moment to Meaning: The Art of Scholar-Practitioner Inquiry*. She is co-founder of the Scholar-Practitioner Nexus, a website focusing on resources to promote practice-embedded, scholarly inquiry.

I was introduced to the concept of clinical supervision through doctoral courses I took with Morris Cogan and Noreen Garman at the University of Pittsburgh. At the time, I was involved with efforts to improve the quality of pre-hospital emergency medical services. These efforts included developing instructor-training programs to prepare skilled emergency medical technicians (EMTs) as teachers. I was drawn to Cogan's rationale for supervision, because at its heart, there seemed to be a great respect for teachers, an honoring of the expertise they brought to their work. Far from a "power-over" imposition of "corrective" prescriptions, supervision was a collaboration toward mutual goals of excellence in teaching. Working in an arena where standards for pre-hospital care and the certification of EMTs were in their infancy, establishing trust and inviting cooperation were essential if any progress was to be made. Clinical supervision (as well as curriculum) opened my eyes to a whole different way of thinking about education.

Although subsequent professional interests took me away from the formal study of supervision, my on-going conversations with Noreen Garman and Helen Hazi allowed me to lurk at the edges of the field. It was disconcerting to hear the elegance of Cogan's rationale reduced to a series of simplistic steps in the name of efficiency. Even more heartbreaking was the imposition of generic checklists that could not remotely capture the complexities of instruction (e.g., Garman & Hazi, 1988). And, in an even more perverse turn, the checklists were touted as objective data in support of legislative efforts to control teaching and supervision (e.g., Hazi & Garman, 1988) as well as to impose draconian accountability measures on both teachers and supervisors (e.g., Muller, 2018).

Thus, it was with some misgivings, I entered into this COPIS project. What could I as an outsider offer to those who deal daily with the complicated terrain of supervision? Yet, I am pleased that I did, for it gave me an opportunity to gain insights into the current state of the field. Of particular interest to me was the rich array of questions that think piece authors posed for deliberation. If one hallmark of a field of study is a shared sense of what questions are worth examining, then the think pieces offer what might be loosely considered a potential research agenda for supervision. Such an agenda might be useful to those contemplating topics for their dissertations, because this next generation of scholars have an opportunity to serve as stewards of the field. As Virginia Richardson (2006) explains:

> ...stewards are able to generate new knowledge,
> understand the intellectual history of the field, use the

best ideas and practice in current work, and represent
that knowledge to others, both within and outside the
field. (p. 251)

Dissertation research has the potential to serve just such intellectual
purposes. In light of this, I share some reflections on potential avenues
for investigation. These are by no means exhaustive, and in many
cases, issues overlap. So, in the evocative spirit of think pieces, I offer
the following.

What's the view?

If one assumes that supervision is a field of study, it seems logical to
ask: What are its boundaries? Which matters are germane to the field
and which are extraneous? Who is within the field and who are the
outsiders? And who gets to decide the answers to such questions?
Posing such questions carries the implication that there can and
should be definitive answers. Yet, in an age where interdisciplinarity
has eroded territorial boundaries between bodies of knowledge, clear
demarcations are inevitably elusive.

As Rebecca Buchanan points out in her think piece, supervision
exists as an edge community at the intersection of multiple boundaries.
And where and how those boundaries are situated depends a great deal
on the perspective of the one mapping the terrain. In this regard, it
may be useful to visualize a map with multiple overlays. For example,
certain features of the field may be more prominent when seen from
the vantage point of teacher education, or educational administration,
or instructional supervision. Different features may come to the
foreground when the field is viewed by those who teach supervision
versus those who are engaged in its practice.

If issues are presented from one taken-for-granted perspective, the
terrain is rather flat and, perhaps, only marginally interesting. When
issues are examined from multiple perspectives, contours of the terrain
become more apparent. It is precisely these contours that present the
most fertile ground for study. So, a key question of the field would
seem to be, "In what ways can we (scholars and practitioners in the
field of supervision), work collaboratively with those in other fields

to generate knowledge that can inform all of our efforts to assure the provision of quality education? Subsumed under this umbrella are questions such as:

- Is it useful/important to consider supervision as a field of study?

- If supervision is a field of study, what are its distinguishing features (e.g., history, knowledge base, influential scholars, shared questions of inquiry)?

- If supervision is considered one function under a broader umbrella of educational administration, then what is the nature and scope of that function (e.g., teacher development, instructional improvement, personnel evaluation)?

- If supervision is a specialized field of practice, what knowledge bases inform that practice?

What's in a name?

The terms "supervisor," "instructional supervision," "educational supervision," "mentoring," and "coaching" are examples of what Mieke Bal (2002) calls "traveling concepts." As she says:

> …concepts are not fixed. They travel—between
> disciplines, between individual scholars, between
> historical periods, and between geographically
> dispersed academic communities. Between disciplines,
> their meaning, reach, and operational value differ.
> (p. 24)

Confusion arises when scholars assume that the meaning they ascribe to a particular concept is universally understood and shared. For decades, "supervision" has been a troubling and troublesome term, leading some to abandon it in favor of terms like "mentoring" or "coaching" or modifying it with adjectives like "instructional" or "educational." Doing so has certain pragmatic value in the world of supervisory practice. Yet, when supervision becomes the focus of scholarly inquiry, what might be lost or gained by glossing over the term's history as it has traveled among disciplines and academic communities?

Cogan had specific reasons for choosing the term *"clinical* supervision" to describe the type of work he and others were doing with neophyte teachers at Harvard and the University of Pittsburgh. He was impressed by the way in which physicians hone their knowledge and craft in the clinical setting, under the tutelage of senior medical staff. As he worked intensively with groups of teachers and student supervisors in school settings, the analogy to supervision in a clinical context might have been useful. Over the years, however, many scholars have replaced "clinical" with "educational" or "instructional." The rationales for alternative terminology are a part of the field's history and provide a context for examining current conceptions of the field. How the field is named situates it in within discourse communities and has implications for the field's purpose. Consider, for example, the following types of questions:

- What are the nuances of meaning among "clinical supervision," "educational supervision," and "instructional supervision," and administrative supervision?

- What purposes, theoretical knowledge, and responsibilities lie at the intersections among the fields of supervision, teacher education, educational administration, and personnel evaluation?

- What questions of significance bear collaborative study by scholars in these fields?

- What, if anything, distinguishes the roles of supervisor, mentor, and coach?

- What are the consequences/tradeoffs of substituting one role descriptor for another or using them interchangeably?

- If supervision is reframed as coaching or mentoring, does that essentially eliminate supervision as a field of study and, if so, what are the implications?

- If supervision is reframed as coaching or mentoring, what term would be appropriate for those with responsibility for creating and maintaining systems that positively or negatively impact the work of teachers?

What's a supervisor to do?

Embedded in debates about the proper designation of the field is an underlying concern about the purpose of supervision. Some see its purpose as supporting the instructional effectiveness of teachers. Others emphasize (and often reject) its role in personnel evaluation. Those outside the field (e.g., policy makers, the general public) see it as a way of forcing compliance with regulations or promoting a particular ideological agenda. Consider the purpose of supervision in relation to just a sampling of issues:

- Promotion of social justice, educational equity, and cultural pluralism;
- Teacher preparation, recruitment, and retention in rural, inner city, economically disadvantaged communities;
- The hiring of underprepared and underqualified individuals to ameliorate teacher shortages;
- Alternative pathways for teacher certification;
- Intelligent Accountability;
- Chronic student absenteeism in the aftermath of the COVID-19 pandemic;
- Technology in the service of instruction, and
- Technology in the service of supervision.

Such issues are complicated and require a level of study and analysis that many teachers and administrators have neither the time nor inclination to investigate in great depth. All too often, this leads to a "quick fix" mentality in which a superficial understanding of what "the research says" leads to wasted time and energy, or worse, harm to students (e.g., Singal, 2021). This complicated and often contested terrain gives rise to three fundamental questions:

- What is the role, responsibility, and ethical duty of supervisors in relation to any given issue?
- What educational preparation and support do supervisors need in order to fulfill their role, responsibilities, and duty?

- In what ways can/should these issues be studied?

In contemplating these questions, the role of the supervisor might be variously framed as:

- Working with individual teachers or groups of teachers to incorporate desired knowledge and skills into their practice;

- Working for systemic change within schools/districts;

- Analyzing the potential consequences of particular policy or program initiatives and preparing concept or position papers to inform decisions of policy and practice; and/or

- Buffering teachers (and school systems) from the effects of counterproductive policies.

For those like doctoral students who are conceptualizing possible research projects, these various features can help to frame a substantive study and to make clear the nature of its scholarly contribution to the field of supervision.

Figure: Framing Studies within the Field of Supervision

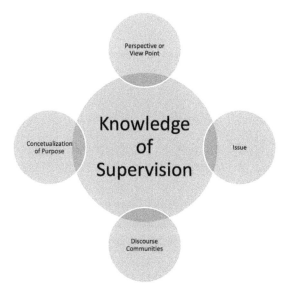

What counts as knowledge of supervision?

The reflections outlined above are meant to highlight a range of issues that impact supervision as a field of study. As someone on the edge of the field, I am in no position to argue that any one particular issue is more important or pressing than others. I do want to argue, however, that thinking about these issues, debating them, and most of all studying them lies at the heart of supervision—if it is to be considered a field of study. This consideration suggests another set of questions deserving attention:

- What forms of research/inquiry most productively serve the field of supervision?

- What is the supervisor's role/responsibility in helping teachers to develop inquiry skills and to use those skills to study their own practice?

- What inquiry skills do supervisors need in order to study their own practice?

- What is gained and what is lost by studying supervision within various theoretical frameworks (e.g., clinical supervision, critical theory, adult development professional development/ expertise)?

If there is merit in deliberating about such matters, what role can COPIS play?

What's COPIS about?

Originally founded by and for professors of supervision, COPIS has broadened its membership to include professors in teacher education programs and practicing supervisors. With such diversity of membership comes the possibility of meaningful deliberation about the issues outlined above. One key issue concerns the organization's role in advocating for certain issues or positions. On one hand, there may be reluctance to embrace this role, for it pulls the field more directly into the political arena. Whether this is ever an attractive prospect, it is certainly cause for pause in this particularly virulent political climate.

On the other hand, our educational institutions are in dire straits. Are those who have deeply studied the role of supervision aptly suited to serve as advocates? This leads to a final question, "What is the relationship between advocacy and stewardship, and what is the field of supervision's duty of care for those whose lives are so forcefully impacted by education?

References

Bal, M. (2002). *Traveling concepts in the humanities: A rough guide*. University of Toronto Press.

Garman, Noreen B. and Helen M. Hazi. "Teachers ask is there life after Madeline Hunter? *Phi Delta Kappan* 69, no. 9 (1988): 669-672.

Hazi, Helen and Noreen B. Garman. "Legalizing scientism through teacher evaluation," *Journal of Personnel Evaluation in Education,* 2, (1988): 1–18.

Muller, J.Z. (2018). *The tyranny of metrics*. Princeton University Press.

Richardson, V. (2006). "Stewards of a field, Stewards of an enterprise." In C.M. Golde & G.E. Walker (Eds), *Envisioning the future of doctoral education: Preparing stewards of the discipline* (pp. 251-267). Jossey-Bass.

Singal, J. (2021). *The quick fix: Why fad psychology can't cure our social ills*. Picador.

Reflections

Duncan Waite

Welcome, dear reader. Whether you're an old hand or a student, school-based, or simply supervision-curious, there's sure to be something here that will speak to you and your interests. The editors of this volume have done a remarkable job in assembling some top thinkers, practitioner-scholars who have been teaching, studying, and practicing supervision for years, in many cases decades. Their contributions here are far-ranging, insightful, reflective, and provocative.

Supervision is concerned above all else with supporting teachers. True, what form that takes is a topic of debate—some of the perspectives are reflected here. Some believe supervision goes beyond simply supporting teachers one-on-one to include curriculum development, and staff development, in addition to instructional improvement. One can readily see how staff and curriculum development go hand-in-glove in support of teachers and their instruction. Others have extended supervision's mandate further and in other directions. Supervision shares certain features with other teacher support efforts such as mentoring and coaching; so much so, that some consider them synonymous. True, though certain tenets, perhaps certain practices, are the same or similar among them, supervision's distinguishing feature is in its clinical manifestation or approach (i.e., clinical in the sense of working in the clinic of practice—the classroom). The distinguishing features of clinical supervision are its cycle of a pre-observation conference, followed by an observation, followed by a post-observation conference. Full disclosure: I myself was brought up in the clinical supervision tradition.

Why does it matter what you call it? It matters not due to issues of methodological, theoretical, or historical fidelity or purity, though there is that. Supervision scholars have argued these issues since its inception. Why it really matters is that the name, and by implication its practices and intents, have been and continue to be coopted, appropriated, and subverted in service of ends that are anathema to its original ideals, those being service to and support of teachers. In those cases, "supervision" has been used as a cover for surveillance, control and regimentation, and the disciplining of teachers.

In the current environment, supervision as it's *supposed* to be practiced becomes a subversive activity. Some time ago, Marilyn Cochran-Smith (1991) wrote of teaching against the grain. Supervision as subversive activity is not dissimilar, though contemporized and solidly situated in the discourse and practice of supervision.

It's all too easy to go astray, lose one's compass when focused chiefly on the details and minutia involved in getting by, day in and day out; especially in such dense and dynamic contexts as schools. Intensification of the teachers' (and supervisors') work is occasioned by increased political pressure—inside and outside of the school; technologies of control evolved way beyond simply "teacher-proofing" the curriculum; and the abandonment of public schools through resource starvation and reallocation in support of private and charter schools (vouchers), resulting in decreased staffing levels and school closures. The demanding nature of teaching, its intensification, makes quick fixes, temporary patches to long-term deep problems seem attractive, practical, or practicable. Not "what works," but whatever works.

It's easy to understand how supervision and supervisors would be drafted into efforts to plug the holes, staunch the bleeding of our severely neglected school system. But if we don't take a step back, see the whole and the trends, reflect and reorient ourselves to our noble mission and fight for it, I fear, like Graber (2018), we will have effectively and "collectively acquiesced to our own enslavement" (p. xxvi), and, I might add, to that of others, those for whom we have a fiduciary responsibility. I believe the choice is that stark: feed the machine or work to subvert it.

In taking a step back, consider our purpose. At the molecular level, supervision is concerned with teacher growth, instructional improvement in the vernacular, though they're not the same thing. Teaching, what is that? Is it only about teaching or might it be about learning? And learning, what is that? It's certainly not quantifiable or measurable. Another step back and we ask questions about learning and schooling, about schooling and education. Education is concerned with human growth—what Wright (2010) terms "human flourishing" and D. H. Lawrence (1950) calls "coming into a fullness of being" free and spontaneous. If we only attend to the technical aspects of schooling, we risk being complicit in simply "raising new generations of workers so that in the future they can, in turn, do the 'real' work of being exploited" (Graeber, 2018, p. 202). This is not an education for a democratic society, for democratic citizens.

Earlier I wrote that a distinguishing feature of (clinical) supervision is the conference-observation-conference cycle, though supervision has a much broader remit, encompassing the whole school and touching the broader community. Long gone are the days when some school personnel were titled "Supervisor," where supervision was their primary job responsibility. Supervision, along with its methods and processes, has become dispersed. What was once the supervisor's job has fractured and fallen to other school personnel—principals, assistant principals, deans of students, coaches, mentors, lead teachers, and more. The reassignment of supervisor tasks and foci has in many cases been hodge-podge, a patchwork, leaving some areas missing altogether.

All this is to say that those of us who believe in supervision must fight to keep it alive, lest it be neglected and forgotten. It also means that volunteers in this fight must come from other positions, those with other job titles. We can't be choosy. We shouldn't allow ourselves to be distracted by territorial, methodological, theoretical quibbles and disagreements, as these can be divisive. It's not an overstatement to suggest that this is a fight for democracy and for education, nothing less. Anyone who's concerned about their own emancipation and that of their charges should be welcome to contribute however they can. Largescale efforts at emancipation are probably off the table—this includes staff development, curriculum improvement, professional development programs, as they'd likely incur repression, and as they are ill-suited to emancipation. Rather, the work of emancipation is organic and spontaneous, often irruptive. The type of emancipation we are concerned with here is best nurtured in relationship, one-to-one, between equals. (It's the same with teachers and students. Rather than lecturing a whole class on emancipation, coming into being, teachers can work the margins, the cracks and crevices of the industrial pedagogical system, to introduce, tease out and foster their and their students' emancipation in relationship.) Supervisors are its ideal agent or actor and supervision conferences the ideal venue. This means that supervisors must work to void their conference interactions of power, authority, or anything that impinges on equality and freedom. It also means that anyone can do it, especially those working closely with teachers—coach, mentor, or whomever. As Lawrence (1950) saw it,

> We know the first great purpose of Democracy: that each man shall be spontaneously himself—each man himself, each woman herself, without any question of equality or inequality entering in at all; and that no man shall try to determine the being of any other man, or any other woman. (p. 93)

Education, emancipation, and democracy should be our aims and supervision their vehicle.

References

Cochran-Smith, M. (1991). Learning to teach against the grain. *Harvard Educational Review, 61*(3), 279-311.

Graeber, D. (2018). *Bullshit jobs: A theory*. Simon & Schuster.

Lawrence, D. H. (1950). Democracy. In *Selected writings* (pp. 73-95). Penguin Books.

Rancière, J. (1991). *The ignorant schoolmaster: Five lessons in intellectual emancipation*. (K. Ross, trans.). Stanford University Press.

Sarason, S. B. (2004). *And what do YOU mean by learning?* Heinemman.

Waite, D. (2022). *On educational leadership as emancipatory practice: Problems and promises*. Routledge.

Wright, E. O. (2010). *E.nvisioning real utopias*. Verso.

INDEX

INDEX

CONCEPTS

Accountability, viii, 11, 16, 22, 30. 33-35, 71-72, 79, 82-85, 164, 176
    intelligent, 78, 80-81, 186
    self, 62, 71-72
Action research, viii, 46, 50-51, 57, 73, 157,
Artificial intelligence, 12, 87
Association for Curriculum and Supervision (ASCD), vii, 31, 143, 151

Best practices, 13-14, 73, 90
Bullshit jobs, 155

Care, 65-66
Coaching, viii, 15, 20, 33, 46, 68, 91-92, 93, 106, 108, 111-112, 114, 118, 122, 124-128, 173, 184-185, 191
Collaborative Autobiography, 73-74
Community, vi-vii, 3, 11-12, 15-17, 20, 23, 29, 35, 47, 61-63, 65, 69-71, 75, 82, 94-99, 102-103, 126, 133, 141-142, 178, 183, 191, 183
Confessional of incompetence, 82
Critical
    conversation, 55
    ethnography/sociology, i
    evaluation, 12
    framework/lens, 21
    friendship, 19
    incidents, 68, 72, 77
    pedagogy, 61
    supervision, v, 60, 62
    theory, 58, 61, 74, 188
Criticality, 22
    incidents
    theory
Cultural pluralism, 134-135, 138, 142, 186
Cultural responsiveness, 68, 72
Curriculum, ii, vii-viii, 13, 27-33, 35, 40, 59-60, 63-64, 107, 110, 125, 135, 141, 148, 157, 161, 182, 191-193

LEARNING MOMENTS PRESS

Learning Moments Press is the publishing arm of the Scholar-Practitioner Nexus, an online community of individuals committed to the quality of education. Learning Moments Press features three series of books.

The Wisdom of Practice Series showcases the work of individuals who illuminate the complexities of practice as they strive to fulfill the purpose of their profession.

The Wisdom of Life Series offers insightful reflections on significant life events that challenge the meaning of one's life, one's sense of self, and one's place in the world.

The Social Context Series showcases the work of individuals who illuminate the macro socio-economic-political contexts within which education policy and practice are enacted.

Cooligraphy artist Daniel Nie created the logo for Learning Moments Press by combining two symbol systems. Following the principles of ancient Asian symbols, Daniel framed the logo with the initials of Learning Moments Press. Within this frame, he has replicated the Adinkra symbol for *Sankofa* as interpreted by graphic artists at the Documents and Design Company. As explained by Wikipedia, Adinkra is a writing system of the Akan culture of West Africa. *Sankofa* symbolizes taking from the past what is good and bringing it into the present in order to make positive progress through the benevolent use of knowledge. Inherent in this philosophy is the belief that the past illuminates the present and that the search for knowledge is a life-long process.

Milton Keynes UK
Ingram Content Group UK Ltd.
UKHW021329280724
446040UK00008B/80